Daily Literacy Activities

20TH CENTURY AMERICAN HISTORY

REM 392

AUTHOR: Sue LaRoy

A TEACHING RESOURCE FROM

©2019
Copyright by Remedia Publications, Inc.
All Rights Reserved. Printed in the U.S.A.

The purchase of this product entitles the individual teacher to reproduce copies for classroom use. The reproduction of any part for an entire school or school system is strictly prohibited.

Some images in this workbook are used under license from Shutterstock.com or through the Ford Motor Company website. All others are public domain images.

www.rempub.com

REMEDIA PUBLICATIONS, INC.
SCOTTSDALE, AZ

This product utilizes innovative strategies and proven methods to improve student learning. The product is based upon reliable research and effective practices that have been replicated in classrooms across the United States. Information regarding the Common Core State Standards this product meets is available at www.rempub.com/standards.

Table of Contents

Teacher Guide		1–3
Story 1	The Industrial Revolution	4-11
Story 2	Immigration	12-19
Story 3	World War I (1914-1918)	20-27
Story 4	Women's Right to Vote	28-35
Story 5	The Roaring Twenties	36-43
Story 6	Hollywood and the Movies!	44-51
Story 7	The Great Depression	52-59
Story 8	World War II in Europe	60-67
Story 9	World War II in the Pacific	68-75
Story 10	America Loves Television	76-83
Story 11	The Space Race	84-91
Story 12	The Civil Rights Movement: Part 1	92-99
Story 13	The Civil Rights Movement: Part 2	100-107
Story 14	The Sixties	108-115
Words to Know		116-118
People and Places		119-121
Enrichment Ideas		122-123
Answer Key		124-127
Notes		128-129
Literacy Book Series		130

Teacher Guide

Literacy means having the ability to read and write. Literacy also means having knowledge or competency in a specified area. The goal of this book is to help students improve reading and writing skills as they learn important information about 20th Century American history. If students can successfully read each story in the book, understand the historical facts presented, and then write about what they have learned, they will have become more literate in American history.

The format of this book lends itself to use with students who are functioning below grade level. The information is presented in a way that allows for differentiated instruction. Teacher understanding of a student's ability level will help determine how much material a student can successfully complete in an allotted time on a daily basis. To help keep track of when each part of the lesson is completed, each page has a line for writing the current date.

BOOK FORMAT

The 14 stories in this book take students on a journey that begins with the Industrial Revolution, moves to The Roaring Twenties, then covers the exciting events of The Space Race, The Civil Rights Movement, and The Sixties. Each three-part story, complete with historical images, is accompanied by five skill-based reading and writing activity pages. These eight pages form a study unit for each story. The stories are numbered to help keep all the story components together.

To encourage students to read and then re-read the text, there is a "locating the information" activity at the bottom of each story page. This simple exercise helps to reinforce key facts from the story. Each story includes words which many students may find challenging. Use of these words is necessary in order to convey historical accuracy. There are three "Words to Know" pages that list difficult or unfamiliar words. Three "People and Places" pages list the names of important people and historic places mentioned in the stories. Two pages of "Enrichment Ideas" offer suggestions for discussion, research, and higher level comprehension questions. The Answer Key provides answers for the comprehension and cloze activity pages.

READABILITY

A specific challenge for this book was being true to history while simplifying the content. An effort was made to create stories that were rich with important historical information, yet on a level that would be understood by those students reading below grade level.

To accomplish this, short sentences, simple explanations, and plenty of repetition was used whenever possible. A reading specialist reviewed the stories for content and reading ease. Use of the historically relevant vocabulary resulted in an average reading level ranging from 5.0 to 6.5 according to the Flesch-Kincaid Scale. The interest level is grade 5 and up.

SUGGESTIONS FOR USE

Start by assembling one of the eight-page study units into a folder with the "Words to Know" and "People and Places" lists for that story. Pre-reading strategies can be used based on each student's needs.

Pre-Reading Strategies

Have the student read the title and study the images on the story pages. Ask the student what the story might be about. On a sheet of paper, make two columns. One labeled "What I Know" and one labeled "What I Want to Know." Anything the student knows about the topic can be written in one column, and anything the student would like to know can be written in the second column. This may pique interest and give the student a reason to read the story. Point out the "Words to Know" and "People and Places" lists that correspond to the story. Ask the student to identify any unfamiliar words. Talk about the historic figures and groups of people mentioned in the story. Offer help with understanding and the pronunciation of difficult words.

Have students create flashcards for difficult words and allow them to work in pairs to master the words. Some students may benefit from learning the definitions of the words and using them in sentences. Dictionary apps are available for a variety of digital devices that allow students to listen to the definition and pronunciation of a word.

To help set the stage for the story, discuss key places referred to where events took place. Many of the topics covered in this book are complex. A general pre-reading discussion may be helpful with some students.

Daily Activities

Daily literacy activities presented in small increments can allow individual students to proceed at their own pace often resulting in a greater understanding of the subject matter.

For example:

Day 1: Student reads the first page of the story and completes the "locating the answer" activity.

Day 2: Student reviews the first page of the story and completes the comprehension questions for that page.

Day 3: Student reads the second page of the story and completes the "locating the answer" activity.

Day 4: Student reviews the second page of the story and completes the comprehension questions for that page.

Day 5: Student reads the third page of the story and completes the "locating the answer" activity.

Day 6: Student reviews the third page of the story and completes the comprehension questions for that page.

Day 7: Student completes the cloze activity and then writes a short summary of the topics listed on the final activity page.

This timeline and the amount of material assigned each day can be adjusted based on skill level. The story sections make excellent homework assignments.

Post-Reading

After completing a study unit, ask students to compare what they have learned with what they wanted to know about the topic. Unanswered questions can stimulate further research.

The two enrichment pages offer ideas to extend learning and help students gain a deeper understanding of the topics in this book.

The Industrial Revolution

Story 1

In the 1700s, a machine was invented that could weave cloth. Workers in big textile mills used these machines. The first American textile mills were built in the Northeast. Water power was used to run the machines. People had always woven cloth by hand. Now, large amounts of cloth could be made at one time. The Industrial Revolution began when textile mills started making cloth. Something that had always been made by hand was now being made by machines.

The Industrial Revolution continued throughout the 1800s and early 1900s. How people lived and worked were changed forever. The steam engine was invented. Railroads were built. Coal and iron mining became big industries. Factories were built to make soap, towels, dishes, and glassware. Hats, shoes, clothing, and perfume were also manufactured in large amounts. There were even big candy factories. People left their farms. They moved to the city to work in factories.

In the early 1900s, electricity was used for the first time to make products. Steel mills were built in the Midwest. Hundreds of other factories were built all over the country. Thousands of jobs were created. The population in factory cities grew quickly. Some cities became overcrowded. Now, more people lived in cities than on farms.

The invention of the automobile and the airplane opened up a whole new world of transportation.

1. Underline the sentence that tells when the Industrial Revolution began.
2. Underline the sentence that tells why people left their farms.
3. Underline the two sentences that tell what happened after thousands of jobs were created.

Name_____ Date_____

Answer the questions with complete sentences.

1. What started the Industrial Revolution?

   _____

   _____

2. Name five things that were made in factories.

   _____

   _____

3. Why did people leave their farms?

   _____

   _____

4. What happened after thousands of jobs were created by steel mills and factories?

   _____

   _____

5. What inventions opened up a whole new world of transportation?

   _____

   _____

The Factory System

Story 1

The factory system was a way to mass-produce products. Before factories, workers made products one at a time. People worked at home or in small workshops. Workers needed special skills to make each product.

Factories used machines powered by steam or electricity to make products. Factories were large buildings where many people gathered to work. The workers ran the machines. They did not need special skills. Workers did not have to know how to make the entire product. They just learned how to make a small piece of the product. Products could be made cheaper, quicker, and in large amounts.

The Moving Assembly Line

In 1913, Henry Ford was the first American to use the moving assembly line. He owned factories that built Ford automobiles. Ford's assembly line moved from one workstation to another. A different part of the car was added at each station. There were 84 stations. By the last station, a Model T Ford had been built! A worker stood at each workstation and did the same job over and over. It was very boring. But Ford made it worthwhile for his workers. He paid them a very good wage. Ford was not like most factory owners. He treated his workers fairly.

It used to take over 12 hours to make a Model T Ford. With the assembly line, it took under two hours. Ford could make cars faster. He could charge less for them. Soon, other kinds of factories started making products in the same way.

1. Underline the sentence that tells how products were made before factories.
2. Underline the sentence that tells who was the first American to use the moving assembly line.
3. Underline the sentence that tells how long it used to take to make a Model T Ford.

Name_____ Date_____

Answer the questions with complete sentences.

1. How and where were products made before factories?

   _____

   _____

2. Describe how products were made in a factory.

   _____

   _____

3. Who was the first American to use the moving assembly line?

   _____

   _____

4. What happened at each workstation in Ford's assembly line?

   _____

   _____

5. How long did it take to make a Model T before the assembly line? How long did it take using the assembly line?

   _____

   _____

Women and Children in Factories

Women were hired to work in some of the factories. Factory owners liked to hire women. They could pay women less money. Men were paid twice as much as women for doing the same job. Most women had never worked outside the home. For the first time, women had their own money. They had a new kind of freedom and independence.

Some poor families sent children to work in the factories. The children were not paid very much. But the families needed the children's wages to survive. The women and children often worked 10 to 12 hour days. The working conditions were terrible. The factory rooms were hot, dirty, crowded, and very noisy. The machines were unsafe. It was a very hard and dangerous life for a child.

Labor Unions

The bad working conditions caused many workers to get sick. Some workers were injured or even killed in workplace accidents. It was not safe to work in most factories. The factory owners did not care about their workers. They did not want to spend money to improve working conditions. They did not want to pay higher wages.

The workers decided to come together and stand up to the factory owners. They formed groups called labor unions. Labor unions gave workers a voice. The unions demanded better pay and safer working conditions. Sometimes the workers had to go on strike. Being on strike meant that work stopped until the owners agreed to make some changes. Slowly, conditions improved in the factories.

1. Underline the sentence that tells why factory owners liked to hire women.
2. Underline the sentence that tells why poor families sent children to work in factories.
3. Underline the two sentences that tell what labor unions did.

Name_____ Date_____

Answer the questions with complete sentences.

1. Why did factory owners like to hire women?

   _____

   _____

2. Why did some poor families send their children to work in factories?

   _____

   _____

3. Describe the working conditions in the factories.

   _____

   _____

4. What happened to some of the workers because of the bad working conditions?

   _____

   _____

5. What did the labor unions do for the workers?

   _____

   _____

Name_____ Date_____

Complete each sentence with a word from the box.

> assembly   factories   twice
> Labor   safe   population
> Revolution mass-produce under

1. The Industrial _____ changed how people lived and worked.

2. People moved from the farm to the city to work in _____.

3. The _____ in factory cities grew quickly.

4. The factory system was a way to _____ products.

5. Ford's _____ line moved from one workstation to another.

6. Model T Ford's could be made in _____ two hours.

7. Men were paid _____ as much as women to do the same job.

8. It was not _____ to work in most factories.

9. _____ unions gave workers a voice.

Read each completed sentence to make sure it makes sense.

Name_____ Date_____

Write two or more sentences about each topic.

The Factory System

_____
_____
_____

The Moving Assembly Line

_____
_____
_____

Labor Unions

_____
_____
_____

Immigration

Story 2

European Immigrants

America is a nation of immigrants. Immigrants are people who leave the country where they were born to live in a new country. Throughout the 1800s, millions of immigrants poured into America. They came from Great Britain, Ireland, and Germany. Many of these people spoke English. They became farmers and businessmen. They helped to build new cities. America grew and became successful. It was the beginning of the American way of life.

It's hard to leave your home country. But sometimes people feel they have no choice. In the early 1900s, there were wars in Europe. The wars destroyed cities and homes. There were too many people and not enough jobs. There was widespread poverty. The wars and poverty affected many people. It was a challenge to survive. Some people were not free to practice their religion.

Word spread throughout Europe that there were jobs in America. There was religious freedom. People were desperate. America offered hope for a better life.

Between 1900 and 1915, about 15 million immigrants came to America. These new immigrants were mostly from Italy, Russia, and Poland. These people did not speak English. Their way of life was much different than life in America. They had a hard time getting used to their new country.

1. Underline the sentence that tells what immigrants are.
2. Underline the sentence that tells where the immigrants that poured into America during the 1800s came from.
3. Underline the sentence that tells how many immigrants came to America between 1900 and 1915.

Name_____ Date_____

Answer the questions with complete sentences.

1. What is an immigrant?

   _____

   _____

2. During the 1800s, where did the immigrants come from?

   _____

   _____

3. Name two reasons people leave their home countries.

   _____

   _____

4. Why did people come to America?

   _____

   _____

5. How many immigrants came to America between 1900 and 1915?

   _____

   _____

Story 2

Ellis Island

Ellis Island was the main immigration station in the United States. It opened in 1892 and closed in 1954. Ellis Island is on the Hudson River between New York and New Jersey. Most European immigrants had to go through Ellis Island.

The immigrants came by ship. They had a long, difficult journey across the ocean. People were afraid when they arrived. They didn't know if they would be allowed to stay. The immigrants had to get permission to enter the U.S. Each person had to answer questions. Everyone had to get a medical exam. If you were not healthy, you could not stay.

The lines to get into the U.S. were very long. It took hours to get through. Some people were held for days or weeks. They had to stay on Ellis Island. They had to wait until a decision was made. In the early 1900s, between 5,000 and 10,000 people came to Ellis Island every day!

Traveling to America was expensive. Some people had to sell all their belongings to get passage on a ship. For these people, there was no going back. It was a matter of survival to be allowed into America. Most people were allowed to stay. Only about 2% of the immigrants were turned away.

In 1924, the Immigration Act was passed. This limited how many people could come to America from each country.

1. Underline the sentence that tells where Ellis Island is located.
2. Underline the three sentences that tell what immigrants had to do to enter the U.S.
3. Underline the sentence that tells how many people came to Ellis Island every day.

Name_____ Date_____

Answer the questions with complete sentences.

1. Where was Ellis Island located?

   _____
   _____

2. Why were people afraid when they arrived in America?

   _____
   _____

3. What did people have to do to enter the U.S.?

   _____
   _____

4. How many people came to Ellis Island every day?

   _____
   _____

5. What happened after the Immigration Act was passed?

   _____
   _____

Story 2

Immigrant Life

Thousands of immigrants stayed in New York City. They gathered in their own neighborhoods. The neighborhoods were very crowded. There could be as many as 4,000 immigrants per block. Most immigrants were poor. They could only afford to live in rundown apartments. These overcrowded apartment buildings were called tenements. Each apartment had three rooms. It had a small living room, a kitchen, and a tiny bedroom. Sometimes, seven or more people lived in each apartment. Until 1905, there were no bathrooms inside the building. There was no electricity until after 1918.

There were plenty of jobs in New York City. But many of the immigrants had no skills. They could not speak English. They could only get low-paying jobs in sweatshops. The working conditions were terrible. Sweatshops were dirty, dingy places with no windows. The workers could not talk or take breaks. They worked long hours. If workers complained, they got fired.

Chinese Immigrants

The first Chinese immigrants came to America in the mid-1800s. Chinese men came to work in the gold mines. They came to help build the railroad. The men left China because they were starving. Americans didn't like the Chinese. They didn't like how the Chinese looked and talked. The Chinese were treated badly. Many were sent home after the railroad was built. In 1882, a law was passed. It said only a small number of Chinese could come into America each year.

The immigrants who came to America are ancestors of today's citizens. Their courage, hard work, and determination helped make America a wealthy and powerful country.

1. Underline the sentence that tells how many immigrants there could be per block.
2. Underline the two sentences that tell why immigrants could only get low-paying jobs in sweatshops.
3. Underline the sentence that tells when the first Chinese immigrants came to America.

Name_____ Date_____

Answer the questions with complete sentences.

1. In the immigrant neighborhoods, how many immigrants were there per block?

   _____
   _____

2. Describe an apartment in a tenement building.

   _____
   _____

3. Why could immigrants only get low-paying jobs in sweatshops?

   _____
   _____

4. What were sweatshops like?

   _____
   _____

5. Why didn't Americans like the Chinese?

   _____
   _____

Name_____ Date_____

Complete each sentence with a word from the box.

```
station      into         spread
afraid       immigrants   dingy
crowded      poverty      treated
```

1. Throughout the 1800s, millions of _____ poured into America.

2. People leave their home countries because of war and _____.

3. Word _____ that there were jobs in America.

4. Ellis Island was the main immigration _____.

5. Immigrants were _____ when they arrived in America.

6. The lines to get _____ the U.S. were very long.

7. Immigrant neighborhoods were very _____.

8. Sweatshops were dirty, _____ places with no windows.

9. Chinese immigrants were _____ badly.

Read each completed sentence to make sure it makes sense.

Name_____ Date_____

Write two or more sentences about each topic.

Ellis Island

_____
_____
_____
_____

Sweatshops

_____
_____
_____
_____

Chinese Immigrants

_____
_____
_____
_____

World War I (1914-1918)

Story 3

World War I was a war between the "old powers" of Europe. On one side was Germany and Austria-Hungary. These countries were the main Central Powers. On the other side was Great Britain, France, and Russia. These were the main countries of the Allied Powers. World War I was also called the "War to End All Wars", the "First World War", and the "Great War."

Causes of the War

For a long time, the old powers of Europe had been in a contest with each other. Each country wanted to be the most powerful. They competed for new lands to rule. In the early 1900s, Great Britain ruled 56 colonies. The British Empire was the largest and most powerful empire in the world. Germany, France, and Russia were also powerful countries.

Great Britain, France, and Russia were allies. Allies are friends who promise to help each other. They promise to fight together. Germany was not a friend of these allies. Germany wanted to be more powerful than Great Britain. This caused tension between Germany and the other countries.

Austria-Hungary ruled the country of Bosnia. In June of 1914, Archduke Franz Ferdinand made an official visit to Bosnia. His wife Sophie was with him. The Archduke was the future king of Austria-Hungary. During the visit, a man from Serbia killed the Archduke and his wife. The government of Austria-Hungary was furious. They blamed the government of Serbia for these deaths. Serbia thought this was unfair. Germany took Austria-Hungary's side. Russia took Serbia's side.

1. Underline the two sentences that list the main countries of the Central Powers and the Allied Powers.
2. Underline the two sentences that tell what allies are.
3. Underline the sentence that tells what happened to the Archduke and his wife while they were visiting Bosnia.

Name_____ Date_____

Answer the questions with complete sentences.

1. Which countries were the main Central Powers? Which countries were the main Allied Powers?

   _____

   _____

2. Why had the old powers of Europe been in a contest with each other?

   _____

   _____

3. What does it mean for countries to be allies?

   _____

   _____

4. What happened to the Archduke and his wife while they were visiting Bosnia?

   _____

   _____

5. Who took Austria-Hungary's side? Who took Serbia's side?

   _____

   _____

Story 3

The War Begins

On July 28, 1914, Austria-Hungary declared war on Serbia. This set off a quick chain of events. Soon other countries were declaring war. Germany declared war on Russia. Then Germany declared war on France. Germany wanted to rule France. Great Britain supported France. They wanted to stop Germany. Great Britain declared war on Germany.

By August of 1914, the two groups were fighting against each other. It was the Central Powers against the Allied Powers. World War I had begun!

In 1914, Woodrow Wilson was president of the United States. President Wilson did not want the U.S. to take sides in the war. The American people did not want to fight a war in Europe. However, many Americans sided with the Allied Powers. Private businesses wanted to help. They loaned large sums of money to the Allied countries.

A New Kind of War: On Land, in the Air, and at Sea

The military used new weapons in World War I. On land, machine guns, tanks, flamethrowers, and poison gas were used for the first time. Machine guns were also attached to small airplanes. Brave pilots fought each other in the sky. A new type of German plane dropped bombs on British and French cities. At sea, submarines hid under the water. In sneak attacks, they used torpedoes to sink enemy ships.

1. Underline the sentence that tells when Austria-Hungary declared war on Serbia.
2. Underline the sentence that tells how private businesses helped the Allied countries.
3. Underline the sentence that tells what new weapons were used on land.

Name_____ Date_____

Answer the questions with complete sentences.

1. When did Austria-Hungary declare war on Serbia?

   _____

   _____

2. Who did Germany declare war on?

   _____

   _____

3. How did President Wilson feel about the war?

   _____

   _____

4. How did American private businesses help the Allied countries?

   _____

   _____

5. What new weapons were used in World War I?

   _____

   _____

America Enters the War

Story 3

German submarines were in the waters around Great Britain. They attacked ships going to and from Great Britain. Germany sank supply ships. But they also sank passenger ships. In 1915, the Germans sank the passenger ship Lusitania. Almost 1,200 men, women, and children died, including 128 Americans.

President Wilson warned Germany to stop sinking passenger ships. He warned them to stop killing Americans. But Germany wanted to win the war. They kept sinking ships. More Americans were killed. The American people were very angry with Germany.

In early 1917, Germany sent a secret telegram to Mexico. Germany asked Mexico to join the Central Powers. They wanted Mexico to fight against America. President Wilson found out about it. He said Germany must be stopped. In April of 1917, America declared war on Germany. The United States had entered World War I. America was on the side of the Allied Powers.

The End of the War

Almost 2 million American soldiers were sent to Europe. America also sent food, weapons, and other supplies. Now, the Allied Powers had a big advantage. They won important battles. In November 1918, Germany stopped fighting. The war was over. The Allied Powers had won! But victory came at a high price. There were huge losses. Over 16 million people died. Countries were torn apart. Many cities were destroyed. It took a long time to repair the damages from the "Great War."

1. Underline the two sentences that tell what President Wilson warned Germany to stop doing.
2. Underline the sentence that tells when America declared war on Germany.
3. Underline the two sentences that tell why the Allied Powers had a big advantage.

Name_____ Date_____

Answer the questions with complete sentences.

1. What did President Wilson warn Germany to stop doing?

   _____

   _____

2. What did the secret telegram say?

   _____

   _____

3. When did America declare war on Germany?

   _____

   _____

4. What did America send to Europe after they entered the war?

   _____

   _____

5. Who won World War I?

   _____

   _____

Name_____ Date_____

Complete each sentence with a word from the box.

> wife   declared   allies
> torpedoes   advantage   tension
> warned   telegram   pilots

1. Great Britain, France, and Russia were _____.

2. There was _____ between Germany and the other countries.

3. The Archduke and his _____ were killed in Bosnia.

4. Austria-Hungary _____ war on Serbia.

5. Brave _____ fought each other in the sky.

6. Submarines used _____ to sink enemy ships.

7. President Wilson _____ Germany to stop sinking passenger ships.

8. Germany sent a secret _____ to Mexico.

9. America gave the Allied Powers a big _____.

Read each completed sentence to make sure it makes sense.

Name_____ Date_____

Write two or more sentences about each topic.

The Central Powers

_____
_____
_____
_____

The Allied Powers

_____
_____
_____
_____

Submarines

_____
_____
_____
_____

Women's Right to Vote

Story 4

Women did not always have the right to vote. That may be hard to believe today. But women have only had the right to vote for about 100 years.

At first, white men who owned land were the only people who could vote. These men voted for people and laws that were helpful to them. Many of the laws were not good for women, poor men or people of color.

After the Civil War, the 15th Amendment to the Constitution was passed. This gave all men, including African-American men, the right to vote. The amendment did not include women. Most states made it very hard for black men to vote. So white men were still making all the laws of the land.

In the 1800s, most men in America believed that women were not their equals. This meant that women had very few rights. They were dependent on men. Women could not own land. They could not earn their own money. Women could not go to college. Wives were often treated like their husband's property. They had to obey their husbands.

Since women could not vote, they had no voice in government. They had no way to pass new laws. Women were being treated unfairly. Only a few brave women were willing to speak out. They demanded equal rights. They demanded the right to vote! However, it would take a long time for this to happen.

1. Underline the sentence that tells how long women have had the right to vote.
2. Underline the sentence that tells what most men in America believed about women.
3. Underline the sentence that tells why women had no voice in government.

Name_____ Date_____

Answer the questions with complete sentences.

1. How long have women had the right to vote?

   _____

   _____

2. What did the 15th Amendment to the Constitution do?

   _____

   _____

3. In the 1800s, what did most men in America believe about women?

   _____

   _____

4. How were wives often treated by their husbands?

   _____

   _____

5. Why didn't women have any voice in government?

   _____

   _____

Name_____ Date_____

Story 4

Women's Suffrage

    Women's suffrage is the right of women to vote in an election. Suffragette's were women who fought for the right to vote. In 1848, the first women's rights convention was held in Seneca Falls, New York. It was led by Lucretia Mott and Elizabeth Cady Stanton. About 300 people came to this first meeting. Most of the people were part of the antislavery movement. But they were also for women's rights. They believed all people should be treated equally.

    A document was written during the convention. It was like a "Declaration of Independence" for women. It said that women should have the same rights as men. Women should be able to vote. This was the beginning of the women's rights movement.

    In 1869, Elizabeth Cady Stanton and Susan B. Anthony formed the National Women's Suffrage Association. This group had one main goal. The goal was to get a law passed that allowed women to vote. This was not a popular idea. Most men did not want women to vote. The suffragettes worked to get these men to change their mind. They gave protest speeches. They marched and picketed for equal rights. But it was dangerous to be a suffragette. They were treated badly. They were yelled at and sometimes got injured. Some suffragettes were even sent to jail.

    In the early 1900s, more women joined the fight. Women were now working in factories. They were making their own money. They were becoming independent. This new group of working women were willing to fight for their rights!

1. Underline the sentence that tells what women's suffrage is.
2. Underline the sentence that tells the main goal of the National Women's Suffrage Association.
3. Underline the three sentences that tell why it was dangerous to be a suffragette.

Name_____ Date_____

Answer the questions with complete sentences.

1. What is women's suffrage?

   _____

   _____

2. Who were the suffragettes?

   _____

   _____

3. What was the main goal of the National Women's Suffrage Association?

   _____

   _____

4. How did men feel about women voting?

   _____

   _____

5. Why was it dangerous to be a suffragette?

   _____

   _____

Name_____ Date_____

Elizabeth Cady Stanton

Story 4

Elizabeth Cady Stanton believed in equal rights for everyone. She fought for an end to slavery. She became one of the first leaders of the women's rights movement. Elizabeth was born into a wealthy family on November 12, 1815. In 1840, Elizabeth married Henry Stanton. Henry also believed in equal rights. Elizabeth had six children. She was a busy wife and mother. Her husband supported her work to help women. She was able to take care of her family and still be a suffragette.

Susan B. Anthony

Susan B. Anthony was famous for her speeches on women's rights. She was born on February 15, 1820. She grew up in a Quaker family. Her family believed that all people were created equal. At a young age, Susan began working with her family to end slavery. Then she got interested in women's suffrage. Susan did not get married. She spent her life working for women's rights.

Susan and Elizabeth worked together for over 50 years. There were many setbacks. But they never gave up. Both women died before their dream of women voting came true.

The 19th Amendment

The 19th Amendment to the Constitution gives all women over the age of 21 the right to vote. The amendment was first sent to Congress in 1878. After 42 years, it was finally passed on August 18, 1920. In November of 1920, millions of women voted for the first time!

1. Underline the sentence that tells why Elizabeth Cady Stanton was able to raise her family and still be a suffragette.
2. Underline the sentence that tells what Susan B. Anthony was famous for.
3. Underline the sentence that tells about the 19th Amendment to the Constitution.

Name_____ Date_____

Answer the questions with complete sentences.

1. Why was Elizabeth Cady Stanton able to take care of her family and still be a suffragette?

   _____

   _____

2. What was Susan B. Anthony famous for?

   _____

   _____

3. How long did Susan and Elizabeth work together?

   _____

   _____

4. What is the 19th Amendment to the Constitution?

   _____

   _____

5. When did women vote for the first time?

   _____

   _____

Name_____ Date_____

Complete each sentence with a word from the box.

> brave   convention   vote
> suffragettes   rights   earn
> protest   working   first

1. Women did not always have the right to _____.

2. Women could not _____ their own money.

3. Only a few _____ women were willing to speak out.

4. The first women's rights _____ was held in 1848.

5. Suffragettes gave _____ speeches.

6. Some _____ were even sent to jail.

7. Elizabeth Cady Stanton believed in equal _____ for everyone.

8. Susan B. Anthony spent her life _____ for women's rights.

9. In November of 1920, millions of women voted for the _____ time!

Read each completed sentence to make sure it makes sense.

Name_____ Date_____

Write two or more sentences about each topic.

Elizabeth Cady Stanton

_____

_____

_____

_____

Susan B. Anthony

_____

_____

_____

_____

Suffragettes

_____

_____

_____

_____

The Roaring Twenties

Story 5

The Roaring Twenties was a nickname for the 1920s. It was an exciting time of change in America. World War I was over and people wanted to enjoy life. They wanted to have fun and be happy. People were willing to try new things. They listened to new kinds of music and tried new dances. They bought new clothes and tried new types of entertainment.

The New Economy

Successful industries had created lots of jobs. Both men and women were working. People had money to spend! For the first time, there was a large group of people with good jobs. They could afford to buy factory-made products. Factory owners got rich selling new inventions. Everyone wanted an electric washing machine, a refrigerator, and a vacuum cleaner. These inventions made life easier.

Banks and businesses started offering credit. People could buy now and pay for it over time. Expensive items like automobiles and radios were often bought on credit. Banks made lots of money when people paid back their loans. The economy was doing great.

New Fashion and Clothing

Both men and women tried the newest fashions in clothing. Men wore pinstriped suits, silk shirts, suspenders, bow ties, and black patent leather shoes. Women's clothing was even more daring. Women had always worn long dresses. They had to wear corsets that were tight and uncomfortable. The new dress styles were loose and comfortable. Women did not need corsets anymore. The dresses had beads, fringe, and pleats. Hemlines were above the knee!

1. Underline the two sentences that tell what new things people were willing to try.
2. Underline the sentence that tells what people with good jobs could afford.
3. Underline the sentence that tells what the new dress styles were like.

Name_____ Date_____

Answer the questions with complete sentences.

1. What kinds of new things were people willing to try in the 1920s?

   _____

   _____

2. Why did people have money to spend?

   _____

   _____

3. Which new inventions made life easier?

   _____

   _____

4. What kind of new clothing did men wear?

   _____

   _____

5. How were the new dress styles different from what women had always worn?

   _____

   _____

Name_____   Date_____

Automobiles

Story 5

Automobiles changed the American way of life. In 1920, the cost of a new Model T Ford was only $260. Now, the average person could afford to own a car. By 1927, 15 million Model T Fords had been sold. Car owners had a new kind of freedom. They could easily take trips. They could travel around the country. Building roads and highways for all these cars created new jobs. New kinds of businesses were created because of the automobile. Cars needed gas stations and auto repair shops. People traveling in cars needed places to stay. Motels were built along the roads and highways.

New Kinds of Entertainment

During the 1920s, people had extra time and money for entertainment. A new invention called movies became popular. There were movie theaters all across the country. It cost between 10 and 25 cents to see a silent movie.

In the early 1920s, the first radio stations were built. The stations broadcast music and the latest news. They also broadcast comedy shows and dramas. The first radios were fancy pieces of furniture. They cost about $150. Families gathered around the radio every day. They listened to their favorite programs. By 1929, about 60% of American homes had a radio.

Baseball also became popular in the 1920s. For the first time, people paid money to watch teams play. Thousands of fans went to baseball games. Fans also listened to the games on the radio.

1. Underline the sentence that tells why the average person could now afford to own a car.
2. Underline the sentence that tells how much it cost to see a silent movie.
3. Underline the two sentences that tell what the first radio stations broadcasted.

Name_____ Date_____

Answer the questions with complete sentences.

1. How much did it cost to buy a Model T Ford in 1920?

   _____

   _____

2. What new invention became popular during the 1920s?

   _____

   _____

3. How much did it cost to see a silent movie?

   _____

   _____

4. What did the first radio stations broadcast?

   _____

   _____

5. What sport became popular in the 1920s?

   _____

   _____

The New Woman

The role of women was changing in America. Women could vote. They could go to college. Some women were working. Some were even learning to drive a car. Flappers were young women who dared to be different. They had new ideas about what it meant to be a woman. Flappers cut their hair short and wore make-up. They dressed in the latest styles. Flappers wore short skirts, feather headbands, and long strings of pearls. They danced in jazz clubs.

The Jazz Age

The Roaring Twenties was also called "The Jazz Age." Jazz was a new kind of music. People hadn't heard anything like it before. Young people loved it! Jazz was played in clubs and on the radio. There were crazy new dances to go along with the new music. The dances had funny names like The Shimmy, The Turkey Trot, The Cake Walk and The Bunny Hop!

The Harlem Renaissance

African-Americans were treated very badly in the South. Segregation made daily life very difficult. For many, it was time to leave the South. Thousands of African-Americans came to Harlem in New York City. Harlem, in the 1920s, became a place of great change for African-Americans. It was a time of modern thinking and new ideas. Musicians, singers, writers, and artists lived in Harlem. They sang and wrote about the hardships in their lives. Amazing art and music was created. Important books were written. Louis Armstrong, Duke Ellington, Bessie Smith, Langston Hughes, Zora Neale Hurston, James Baldwin, and many others became famous during the renaissance.

1. Underline the sentence that tells who dared to be different.
2. Underline the two sentences that tell why it was time for many African-Americans to leave the South.
3. Underline the sentence that tells who became famous during the renaissance.

Name_____ Date_____

Answer the questions with complete sentences.

1. How had things changed for women in America?
   _____
   _____

2. What were young women who dared to be different called?
   _____
   _____

3. What were the names of the crazy new dances?
   _____
   _____

4. Why did many African-Americans feel it was time to leave the South?
   _____
   _____

5. Who were some of the people who became famous during the Harlem Renaissance?
   _____
   _____

Name_____ Date_____

Complete each sentence with a word from the box.

Hemlines	movies	afford
average	Renaissance	Jazz
fancy	credit	wore

1. People with good jobs could _____ to buy factory-made products.

2. Banks and businesses started offering _____.

3. _____ on the new dresses were above the knee!

4. In the 1920s, the _____ person could afford to own a Model T Ford.

5. A new invention called _____ became popular.

6. The first radios were _____ pieces of furniture.

7. The Roaring Twenties was also called the _____ Age.

8. Flappers cut their hair and _____ make-up.

9. Amazing art and music was created during the Harlem _____.

Read each completed sentence to make sure it makes sense.

Name_____ Date_____

Write two or more sentences about each topic.

The First Radios

_____
_____
_____

Flappers

_____
_____
_____

The Harlem Renaissance

_____
_____
_____

Name_____ Date_____

Story 6

Hollywood and the Movies!

Hollywood is the home of the movie industry. It's hard to think of Hollywood without thinking of the magic and glamour of the movies. Hollywood started out as a small California farming community. As it grew, it became part of Los Angeles.

D.W. Griffith filmed the first movie in Hollywood in 1910. It was called *In Old California*. Early movies were filmed outside. Sunlight was used as lighting for the movie set. Hollywood's weather was warm and sunny. There were plenty of wide open spaces. It was the perfect place to film a movie. Soon, other filmmakers were coming to Hollywood.

Silent Movies

The first movies were silent movies. They were filmed in black and white. There were comedies, dramas, westerns, and adventure movies. The first motion picture cameras did not include sound. The actors had to "act out" the story using body language. They also used heavy make-up and dramatic facial expressions. Today, we would think of it as overacting.

The plot of the story was written on title cards. What the actors said was also written on the cards. Before each scene, a title card was shown. The card would tell what happened next. Special music was written for each movie. The music helped to tell the story. It made people feel happy, sad, excited, or afraid. The music was played live in the theater on a piano or organ.

1. Underline the two sentences that tell why Hollywood was the perfect place to film a movie.
2. Underline the sentence that tells about the first motion picture camera.
3. Underline the two sentences that tell what was written on title cards.

Name _____ Date _____

Answer the questions with complete sentences.

1. Why was Hollywood the perfect place to film a movie?

   _____

   _____

2. Why were the first movies silent movies?

   _____

   _____

3. How did actors tell the story in silent movies?

   _____

   _____

4. What was written on the title cards for silent movies?

   _____

   _____

5. How did the special music written for silent movies make people feel?

   _____

   _____

Silent Movie Stars

Two of the most famous silent movie stars were Charlie Chaplin and Mary Pickford. Charlie Chaplin played a character called the "Little Tramp." The Little Tramp had sad eyes and a small mustache. He wore a bowler hat, baggy pants, big shoes, and carried a cane. He could make you laugh or make you cry. The Little Tramp was in movies like *The Kid* and *The Gold Rush*. People around the world loved Charlie Chaplin and his movies. Even the King of England loved the Little Tramp!

Mary Pickford was called "America's Sweetheart." She was known for her long, golden curls. She made dozens of very popular movies playing young, sweet girls. Mary was a smart and talented actress. She was also a good business person. At the time, most actors were not paid very well. But Mary stood up for herself. She demanded more money. During the 1920s, Mary was one of the richest and most famous women in America.

The Talkies

By 1927, movies were being made with sound. These new movies were called "talkies." The first talkie was a movie called *The Jazz Singer*. The actors sang and talked. It became a huge hit. By the early 1930s, most movies were talkies. Some silent movie stars did not do well in the talkies. It was a different kind of acting. A whole new group of movie stars became popular.

1. Underline the sentence that tells who the two most famous silent movie stars were.
2. Underline the sentence that tells what movies with sound were called.
3. Underline the sentence that tells why some silent movie stars did not do well in the talkies.

Name_____ Date_____

Answer the questions with complete sentences.

1. Who were two of the most famous silent movie stars?

   _____

   _____

2. Describe the "Little Tramp" character played by Charlie Chaplin.

   _____

   _____

3. What was Mary Pickford called? What was she known for?

   _____

   _____

4. When movies started being made with sound, what were they called?

   _____

   _____

5. Why did some silent movie stars not do well in the talkies?

   _____

   _____

Story 6

The Golden Age of Hollywood

The 1920s through the 1950s was the Golden Age of Hollywood. Movies were big business. All the major movie studios were in Hollywood. During this time, movies were one of the biggest industries in America. An average of 700 movies were made each year!

People of all ages loved the movies. It was entertainment everyone could afford. A movie cost about 25 cents. There were over 25,000 movie theaters across the country. Each week about 100 million people went to the movies! The movie industry made over $2 billion a year.

The Golden Age of Hollywood was a time of glamorous movie stars and wonderful movies. Everyone had a favorite actor or actress. Clark Gable, Katherine Hepburn, and Cary Grant starred in silly comedies. Fred Astaire and Ginger Rogers became stars dancing in musicals. Gangster movies made James Cagney and Humphrey Bogart famous. Little Shirley Temple was the most popular child star of the 1930s.

In 1939, *Gone with the Wind* and *The Wizard of Oz* were made. Both of these amazing movies were filmed in beautiful "Technicolor." They are still popular today. *Gone with the Wind* is one of the greatest films of all time.

Movies were very popular during the Great Depression. Going to the movies helped people through tough times. At the movies, people could escape their problems. They could lose themselves in another world. Movies became an important part of American culture.

1. Underline the sentence that tells when the Golden Age of Hollywood was.
2. Underline the sentence that tells how many people went to the movies each week.
3. Underline the sentence that tells what movies made in 1939 are still popular today.

Name_____ Date_____

Answer the questions with complete sentences.

1. When was the Golden Age of Hollywood?

   _____

   _____

2. How many movies were made each year?

   _____

   _____

3. How many people went to the movies each week?

   _____

   _____

4. Name four movie stars from the Golden Age of Hollywood.

   _____

   _____

5. What two movies made in 1939 are still popular today?

   _____

   _____

Name_____ Date_____

Complete each sentence with a word from the box.

glamorous	average	perfect
escape	character	movies
expressions	sang	silent

1. Hollywood was the _____ place to film a movie.

2. The first movies were called _____ movies.

3. Silent actors used heavy make-up and dramatic facial _____.

4. Charlie Chaplin played a _____ called the "Little Tramp."

5. Mary Pickford made dozens of very popular _____.

6. In the first talkie movie, the actors _____ and talked.

7. An _____ of 700 movies were made each year.

8. The Golden Age of Hollywood was a time of _____ movie stars.

9. At the movies, people could _____ their problems.

Read each completed sentence to make sure it makes sense.

Name_____ Date_____

Write two or more sentences about each topic.

Silent Movies

_____
_____
_____

Charlie Chaplin

_____
_____
_____

Mary Pickford

_____
_____
_____

Name_____ Date_____

The Great Depression

Story 7

The Great Depression was the worst economic depression in American history. It started in 1929 and lasted through the end of the 1930s. It was a terrible time in America. The stock market crashed. Banks and businesses closed. Farmers in the Southwest lost their farms. Millions of people lost their jobs, their money, and their homes. People felt desperate and afraid. They did not know what to do.

The Stock Market Crash

During the 1920s, the economy was booming. People had extra money to spend. Millions of people put their money in the stock market for the first time. The stock market is a place where people can buy and sell shares of stock in a company. Companies sell shares of stock to get money to run their business. People who buy shares are part owners of that business.

Stock prices for businesses go up and down every day. People in the stock market are buying and selling stocks all the time. When stock prices go up, people make money. When stock prices go down, people lose money.

In October of 1929, thousands of stock prices went down all at once. This caused the stock market to crash. Crowds of worried people gathered outside the New York Stock Exchange. This crash was the beginning of the Great Depression. Most people in the stock market lost all their money. Many companies went out of business.

1. Underline the sentence that tells when the Great Depression took place.
2. Underline the sentence that tells what the stock market is.
3. Underline the sentence that tells what caused the stock market to crash.

Name_____ Date_____

Answer the questions with complete sentences.

1. When was the Great Depression?

   _____

   _____

2. What is the stock market?

   _____

   _____

3. What happens when stock prices go up? What happens when stock prices go down?

   _____

   _____

4. What happened to the stock market in October of 1929?

   _____

   _____

5. What happened to people in the stock market after the crash?

   _____

   _____

Banks and Businesses Close

After the stock market crash, banks began to fail. The banking system was weak. The money in most banks was not protected by the federal government. When a bank closed, the bank's customers lost all their money. The customers got very angry. Hundreds of people would gather outside the bank. They would try to get into the bank and get their money. But the bank would not let them in. Sometimes there were riots in the street. The riots did not help. The money was gone! During the Great Depression, over 9,000 banks closed. Customers lost over $1 billion!

The stock market crash also caused over 300,000 companies to go out of business. All the people who worked for those companies lost their jobs. Suddenly, they had no money to pay their bills or to buy food. They could not find other jobs. By 1933, 25% of Americans were out of work.

Millions of people were hungry and homeless. People traveled from city to city looking for work. Families lived in their cars. Some families did not have a car. Those families walked from city to city. They slept in tents or cardboard boxes. They slept under bridges. Most cities had soup kitchens for the hungry. People waited in long lines to get a little bit to eat.

1. Underline the sentence that tells what happened when a bank closed.
2. Underline the sentence that tells why people suddenly had no money to pay their bills or to buy food.
3. Underline the two sentences that tell what happened to families that did not have a car.

Name_____ Date_____

Answer the questions with complete sentences.

1. What happened when a bank closed?

   _____

   _____

2. How many banks closed during the Great Depression?

   _____

   _____

3. Why did people suddenly have no money to pay their bills or to buy food?

   _____

   _____

4. What happened to families that did not have cars to travel from city to city?

   _____

   _____

5. Why did people have to wait in long lines?

   _____

   _____

Story 7

The Dust Bowl

In the summer of 1931, a long drought started in the Southern Great Plains. A drought is a period of time when there is no rain. This drought lasted until 1939! Five states were hit the hardest. Kansas, Oklahoma, Texas, New Mexico, and Colorado became known as the Dust Bowl.

There were hundreds of farms in these states. Many of the farmers did not take good care of their land. They planted the same crops every year. They did not plant any trees or grass to keep the soil healthy. When the drought came, the soil dried up and turned to dust. The crops died. Now, the farmers had no way of making money.

Strong winds caused huge dust storms. Sometimes the dust was so bad it blocked out the sun. It covered everything. The dust got into homes, schools, and businesses. Some people and animals died from breathing in the dust. During the 1930s, over 2 million people left the Dust Bowl states.

The New Deal

Franklin Delano Roosevelt was elected president in 1932. He wanted the government to help people who had lost their jobs and farms. He had a plan called the New Deal. The New Deal created millions of jobs building bridges and roads across the country. Farmers were put to work planting trees. This helped restore the farm land. The New Deal did not end the Great Depression. But it helped solve some of the problems.

1. Underline the sentence that tells which states became known as the Dust Bowl.
2. Underline the two sentences that tell what happened when the drought came.
3. Underline the sentence that tells what President Roosevelt wanted the government to do.

Name_____ Date_____

Answer the questions with complete sentences.

1. Which states became known as the Dust Bowl?

   _____

   _____

2. What happened when the drought came?

   _____

   _____

3. How many people left the Dust Bowl states during the 1930s?

   _____

   _____

4. What did President Roosevelt want the government to do?

   _____

   _____

5. How did the New Deal help people who were out of work and farmers?

   _____

   _____

Name_____ Date_____

Complete each sentence with a word from the box.

crashed	riots	economic
hungry	companies	money
winds	drought	dried

1. The Great Depression was the worst _____ depression in American history.

2. The stock market _____ in October of 1929.

3. Most people in the stock market lost all their _____.

4. Sometimes there were _____ in the street.

5. Over 300,000 _____ went out of business.

6. Millions of people were _____ and homeless.

7. The _____ lasted until 1939!

8. When the drought came, the soil _____ up and turned to dust.

9. Strong _____ caused huge dust storms.

Read each completed sentence to make sure it makes sense.

Name_____ Date_____

Write two or more sentences about each topic.

The Stock Market

_____
_____
_____

The Dust Bowl

_____
_____
_____

The New Deal

_____
_____
_____

World War II in Europe

Story 8

World War II was the deadliest war in history. Between 60 and 80 million people lost their lives. This included over 6 million Jewish people who were killed by the Nazis. World War II destroyed more cities, homes, and land around the world than any other war.

The war was between the Axis Powers and the Allied Powers. The Axis Powers included Germany, Italy, and Japan. The Allied Powers included Great Britain, the Soviet Union, and France. Later, the United States joined the Allied Powers.

The war lasted for six terrible years. It started in 1939 and ended in 1945. Most of the fighting took place in Europe and parts of Asia. Over 30 countries were included in the war.

Causes of the War in Europe

There was a lot of unrest in Germany. The German people were upset about losing World War I. Also, the Great Depression of the 1930s had spread throughout Europe. Many people had lost their jobs. They did not have enough food to eat. People needed help. They wanted a change. Dictators came into power. They promised jobs and a better life. Benito Mussolini was the dictator of Italy. Adolf Hitler became the dictator of Germany. These two leaders decided to work together. Both men wanted to grow their empires. They wanted to take over other countries. Hitler and Mussolini made a deal to fight together if there was a war.

1. Underline the two sentences that tell who the Axis Powers were and who the Allied Powers were.
2. Underline the sentence that tells how long the war lasted.
3. Underline the sentence that tells who became the dictator of Germany.

Name_____ Date_____

Answer the questions with complete sentences.

1. Which countries were the Axis Powers? Which countries were the Allied Powers?

   _____

   _____

2. How long did World War II last?

   _____

   _____

3. What did dictators promise?

   _____

   _____

4. Who was the dictator of Italy? Who became the dictator of Germany?

   _____

   _____

5. What deal did Hitler and Mussolini make?

   _____

   _____

Adolf Hitler

Story 8

Adolf Hitler was born in Austria in 1889. He fought for Germany in World War I. During the 1920s, Hitler became the leader of Germany's Nazi Party.

Hitler was good at making speeches. The German people liked what he had to say. By 1933, Hitler was Germany's dictator. The Nazi Party ruled Germany. The Nazis believed Germans were better than other people.

Hitler hated the Jewish people. He wanted them out of Germany. He said Jewish people could not be trusted. Hitler believed they caused Germany to lose World War I. He thought Jewish people caused most of Germany's problems. Hitler got the German people to believe this too.

In 1938, Hitler started taking over other countries. Hitler's goal was to control all of Europe.

The War Begins in Europe

On September 1, 1939, Hitler invaded Poland. Great Britain and France were friends with Poland. They had promised to help if Poland was attacked by Germany. On September 3, 1939, Britain and France declared war on Germany. It was the beginning of World War II!

Germany was a powerful enemy. They had an excellent, well-trained Army and Air Force. They had the best military planes and tanks. Germany quickly started bombing Britain and France. They attacked from the air and on land. At the same time, Germany invaded Norway and Denmark.

1. Underline the three sentences that tell why Hitler wanted Jewish people out of Germany.

2. Underline the sentence that tells what happened on September 1, 1939.

3. Underline the sentence that tells what happened after Britain and France declared war on Germany.

Name_____ Date_____

Answer the questions with complete sentences.

1. Name two reasons Hitler wanted Jewish people out of Germany.

   _____

   _____

2. What was Hitler's goal?

   _____

   _____

3. What happened on September 1, 1939?

   _____

   _____

4. Why did Britain and France declare war on Germany?

   _____

   _____

5. Why was Germany a powerful enemy?

   _____

   _____

Name _____ Date _____

Story 8

On June 10, 1940, Italy joined with Germany. Italy declared war on Britain and France. By June 14, Germany had taken over part of France. By 1941, Germany had control over most of Europe. Germany kept bombing Britain. But they were not able to control Britain.

The Holocaust

Hitler wanted to get rid of all the Jewish people in Europe. First, the Nazis would take over a country. Then, the Jewish people in that country were put on trains. They were sent to concentration camps. There were tall fences around the camps. There were Nazi guards. The people were prisoners. Families were split up. Everyone had to work. There was not enough food. Many people died of hunger. People who were sick or couldn't work were killed.

Some concentration camps were "death camps." Everyone sent to a death camp was killed right away. Over 6 million Jewish people died in concentration camps. This horrible time in history is called the Holocaust.

The End of the War in Europe

America entered the war towards the end of 1941. American soldiers were a big help to the Allied forces. In 1942 and 1943, Germany was heavily bombed. The Germans started losing battles. Italy surrendered to the Allies. In June of 1944, the Germans were forced out of France. Germany was losing the war.  On April 30, 1945, Hitler killed himself. Germany surrendered on May 8, 1945. The war in Europe was over! The Allied forces had won!

1. Underline the sentence that tells what happened to Jewish people who were put on trains.
2. Underline the sentence that tells what happened to everyone sent to a death camp.
3. Underline the sentence that tells who won the war in Europe.

Name_____ Date_____

Answer the questions with complete sentences.

1. When did Italy join with Germany in the war?

   _____

   _____

2. What happened to Jewish people after they were put on trains?

   _____

   _____

3. What happened to everyone sent to a death camp?

   _____

   _____

4. How many Jewish people died in concentration camps?

   _____

   _____

5. Who won the war in Europe?

   _____

   _____

Name_____ Date_____

Complete each sentence with a word from the box.

concentration	Dictators	deadliest
Jewish	control	Allied
Germany	sick	declared

1. World War II was the _____ war in history.

2. _____ promised jobs and a better life.

3. Adolf Hitler became the dictator of _____.

4. Hitler hated the _____ people.

5. Hitler's goal was to _____ all of Europe.

6. On September 3, 1939, Britain and France _____ war on Germany.

7. Jewish people were sent to _____ camps.

8. People who were _____ or couldn't work were killed.

9. The _____ forces won the war in Europe!

Read each completed sentence to make sure it makes sense.

Name_____ Date_____

Write two or more sentences about each topic.

Adolf Hitler

_____
_____
_____

Concentration Camps

_____
_____
_____

The Holocaust

_____
_____
_____

World War II in the Pacific

Story 9

World War II was fought in two main parts of the world. The world war in Europe started in 1939. It was fought throughout most of the countries in Europe. The world war in the Pacific didn't start until the end of 1941. It was fought in China, Japan, and Southeast Asia.

Causes of the War in the Pacific

Japan is a small but powerful country. It is an island in the Pacific Ocean. The island is close to China. Japan is about the size of the state of California. In the 1940s, it had a population of about 72 million. Emperor Hirohito was the ruler of Japan during World War II. Hirohito and his military leaders wanted Japan to grow. They wanted to take over other Asian countries.

Japan had a strong military. There were almost 2 million soldiers in the Japanese Army. In 1937, Japan invaded China. They wanted China's land and some of its resources. The Japanese Army marched through the countryside. They destroyed cities and farms. They killed thousands of Chinese people. In 1940, Japan joined Italy and Germany. Japan became one of the Axis Powers. The Axis Powers wanted to rule the world!

The United States did not like what Japan was doing to China. The U.S. stopped selling oil, steel, and other goods to Japan. President Roosevelt told Japan they had to stop attacking China.

1. Underline the sentence that tells when the world war in the Pacific started.
2. Underline the sentence that tells who the ruler of Japan was.
3. Underline the sentence that tells what happened in 1937.

Name_____ Date_____

Answer the questions with complete sentences.

1. When did the world war in the Pacific start?

   _____

   _____

2. Who was the ruler of Japan during World War II?

   _____

   _____

3. What happened in 1937?

   _____

   _____

4. What did the Japanese Army do as they marched through the countryside of China?

   _____

   _____

5. What did the Axis Powers want to do?

   _____

   _____

The Attack on Pearl Harbor

President Roosevelt thought he could make a deal with Japan. Japan needed American oil and steel. Roosevelt thought he could get Japan to stop the attacks on China. But he was wrong. Japan's leaders were very angry with America. Japan would not be stopped.

Hirohito thought America might start a war with Japan. So, he decided to act first. The U.S. Navy had an important naval base at Pearl Harbor, Hawaii. There were many U.S. war ships in the harbor. There were fighter planes in airfields close by. Japan's plan was to destroy these ships and planes. Then, America would not be able to attack Japan.

It was early Sunday morning on December 7, 1941. Over 200 hundred Japanese bombers and fighter planes were in the air. They were secretly on their way to Pearl Harbor. The Japanese planes dropped bombs on the harbor and the airfields at the same time. It was a surprise attack!

The attack lasted less than two hours. Twenty-one U.S. ships were sunk or damaged. Over 180 fighter planes were destroyed. More than 2,400 people were killed during the attack. There were about 1,200 wounded.

America was in shock! No one expected the attack. The next day, America declared war on Japan. Then, Germany declared war on America. Suddenly, America was in World War II!

1. Underline the sentence that tells what was at Pearl Harbor, Hawaii.
2. Underline the sentence that tells where the Japanese dropped bombs.
3. Underline the two sentences that tell how many people were killed or wounded during the attack.

Name_____ Date_____

Answer the questions with complete sentences.

1. What was at Pearl Harbor, Hawaii?

   _____

   _____

2. When did the attack on Pearl Harbor take place?

   _____

   _____

3. Where did the Japanese drop their bombs?

   _____

   _____

4. How many ships were sunk or damaged? How many fighter planes were destroyed?

   _____

   _____

5. What happened the day after the attack?

   _____

   _____

Name_____ Date_____

Story 9

When America entered the war, they joined Great Britain and France. They were fighting against Germany, Italy, and Japan. U.S. troops were sent to Europe to fight the Germans. U.S. battleships and aircraft carriers were sent to the Pacific. They were sent to fight the Japanese.

The War in the Pacific

During 1942, Japan quickly took over several countries and islands in Southeast Asia. Japan was winning every battle they fought. In June 1942, Japan attacked a U.S. base on Midway Island. This time, America won the battle. It was a turning point in the war. America started taking over some islands in the South Pacific. They won a long, hard battle for the island of Iwo Jima. This victory put U.S. troops close to Japan. Japan was losing the war. But they would not give up.

The Atomic Bomb

American leaders thought about invading Japan. But they were afraid too many American soldiers would be killed. Harry Truman became president in April of 1945. He did not want to invade Japan.

Scientists had invented a new weapon called the atomic bomb. It was the most powerful and dangerous bomb ever made. Truman decided to use this bomb on Japan. On August 6, 1945, an atomic bomb destroyed the city of Hiroshima. More than 70,000 people were killed. Japan still would not give up. Another atomic bomb was dropped on the city of Nagasaki. This time, 40,000 people died. Japan finally surrendered! The war in the Pacific was over.

1. Underline the sentence that tells why U.S. battleships and aircraft carriers were sent to the Pacific.
2. Underline the sentence that tells what new weapon scientists had invented.
3. Underline the two sentences that tell why Japan finally surrendered.

Name_____ Date_____

Answer the questions with complete sentences.

1. Why were U.S. battleships and aircraft carriers sent to the Pacific?
   _____
   _____

2. Why didn't American leaders want to invade Japan?
   _____
   _____

3. What was the new weapon that scientists had invented?
   _____
   _____

4. When was the atomic bomb dropped on Hiroshima?
   _____
   _____

5. What made Japan finally surrender?
   _____
   _____

Name_____ Date_____

Complete each sentence with a word from the box.

invaded	destroy	decided
surrendered	atomic	ruler
population	less	next

1. In the 1940s, Japan had a _____ of about 72 million.

2. Emperor Hirohito was the _____ of Japan during World War II.

3. Japan _____ China in 1937.

4. Japan's plan was to _____ the ships and planes at Pearl Harbor.

5. The attack on Pearl Harbor lasted _____ than two hours.

6. The _____ day, America declared war on Japan.

7. Scientists invented a new weapon called the _____ bomb.

8. President Truman _____ to use the atomic bomb on Japan.

9. Japan finally _____ after an atomic bomb was dropped on Nagasaki.

Read each completed sentence to make sure it makes sense.

Name_____ Date_____

Write two or more sentences about each topic.

Japan

_____
_____
_____
_____

Pearl Harbor

_____
_____
_____
_____

The Atomic Bomb

_____
_____
_____
_____

Name_____ Date_____

Story 10

America Loves Television

Americans first saw television in the late 1940s. It was love at first sight! People were fascinated by what they called "radio with pictures." The first television sets were expensive. They cost about $500. Not many people could afford their own television. In 1953, the cost went down. Televisions cost about $200. By 1955, half of all American homes had TV sets!

During the 1950s, most TV shows were filmed in black and white. The first television sets were made to show black and white programs. By the early 1960s, many programs were being filmed in color. Color TVs cost more money. Many people kept their black and white sets. It took awhile for people to change to color. Most people didn't have color TVs until the end of the 1970s.

Television caught on quickly. Soon, it was the most popular type of entertainment. People could watch it from the comfort of their homes. Watching TV had a huge effect on the American way of life. Kids sat in front of the TV for several hours a day. Families came together to watch their favorite shows. Television brought the whole country closer together. Millions of people were watching the same show at the same time. This gave people from different places something in common.

1. Underline the sentence that tells how much the first television sets cost.
2. Underline the sentence that tells how most TV shows were filmed during the 1950s.
3. Underline the sentence that tells what had a huge effect on the American way of life.

Name_____ Date_____

Answer the questions with complete sentences.

1. How much did the first television sets cost?

   _____

   _____

2. How many American homes had TV sets by 1955?

   _____

   _____

3. During the 1950s, how were most TV shows filmed?

   _____

   _____

4. What had a huge effect on the American way of life?

   _____

   _____

5. Why did television bring the whole country closer together?

   _____

   _____

Television Networks

There were only three major networks when television first started. CBS and NBC had been very successful in radio. So, they decided to try television. Shows like *The Lone Ranger, The Adventures of Superman, Gunsmoke,* and *Perry Mason* started out as radio programs. Then, they became popular TV shows. ABC was the third network.

Television broadcasting started at about 10:00 each morning. The networks signed off every night at about 11:00. There was no broadcasting overnight. It was a challenge for the networks to create enough shows to fill the schedule. During the day, there were kids shows, soap operas, game shows, and talk shows. Evening started out with the news. Later, there were variety shows, westerns, comedies, and dramas.

TV Advertising

Television was an amazing new way for companies to advertise their products. They could reach millions of people at the same time. Companies paid a high price to show their commercials. Networks made a lot of money from advertisers. Some of that money went towards making new shows.

Commercials are short films about a product. They show how a product can be used. Commercials tell viewers why they should buy a certain product. Some commercials used celebrities and cartoon characters. Many commercials had silly songs. People remembered these songs and bought the product. Companies had commercials for everything from cars to cereal to toothpaste. TV was a very successful way of advertising!

1. Underline the sentence that tells what shows started out as radio programs.
2. Underline the two sentences that tell when television broadcasting started and when the networks signed off.
3. Underline the sentence that tells why television was an amazing new way for companies to advertise their products.

Name_____ Date_____

Answer the questions with complete sentences.

1. What were the three major networks when television first started?

   _____
   _____

2. When did television broadcasting start each morning? When did networks sign off each night?

   _____
   _____

3. What kinds of shows were on during the day?

   _____
   _____

4. What kinds of shows were on in the evening?

   _____
   _____

5. Why was television an amazing new way for companies to advertise their products?

   _____
   _____

Name_____ Date_____

The Golden Age of Television

Story 10

The 1950s is called the Golden Age of Television. Television was a new kind of entertainment. Networks had to be creative. They had to make different types of shows. They needed to keep people interested. Most shows were broadcast live. This was a big challenge for the actors. But it was exciting for viewers. Anything could happen!

Television changed how America got their news. Some news was shown as it was happening. People felt more connected to the news of the day. Television also changed how America chose its president. In 1952, Dwight Eisenhower was running for president. He was the first candidate to make commercials. This made a big difference when it came time to vote.

Kids watched cartoons and shows like *Howdy Doody, Captain Kangaroo,* and *The Mickey Mouse Club*. The most popular comedy show was *I Love Lucy*. Lucy made everyone laugh with her wacky adventures. People truly did "love Lucy!" People also loved Westerns. There were

plenty of Western heroes, including *The Lone Ranger* and *Davy Crockett*. By the end of the 1950s, there were over 30 Westerns on each week. One of the most popular Westerns was *Gunsmoke*. It was on for 20 years!

By 1965, 94% of American homes had at least one television set. Television became an important part of most people's daily life.

1. Underline the sentence that tells how most shows were broadcast.
2. Underline the sentence that tells what the most popular comedy show was.
3. Underline the sentence that tells how many Westerns were on each week.

Name_____ Date_____

Answer the questions with complete sentences.

1. How were most shows broadcast during the Golden Age of Television?

   _____

   _____

2. Who was the first candidate to make commercials?

   _____

   _____

3. What was the most popular comedy show?

   _____

   _____

4. By the end of the 1950s, how many Westerns were on each week?

   _____

   _____

5. By 1965, how many American homes had at least one television set?

   _____

   _____

Name_____ Date_____

Complete each sentence with a word from the box.

viewers	filmed	cost
advertising	Commercials	networks
television	daily	Westerns

1. In 1953, television sets _____ about $200.

2. TV shows were _____ in black and white in the 1950s.

3. Soon, _____ was the most popular type of entertainment.

4. There were only three major _____ when television first started.

5. _____ are short films about a product.

6. TV was a very successful way of _____.

7. Live shows were exciting for _____.

8. One of the most popular _____ was *Gunsmoke*.

9. Television became an important part of most people's _____ life.

Read each completed sentence to make sure it makes sense.

Name_____ Date_____

Write two or more sentences about each topic.

Television Networks

_____

_____

_____

_____

TV Commercials

_____

_____

_____

_____

TV Westerns

_____

_____

_____

_____

The Space Race

Story 11

The Cold War

After World War II, there was a new conflict. It was called the Cold War. The Cold War was between the United States and the Soviet Union. They were the two most powerful nations in the world. There was no actual fighting. But the two countries were enemies. They were in competition with each other. They spied on each other. The Space Race was part of the Cold War. The Space Race began in 1955. Each country wanted to have the best space technology. Space was the "next frontier." Each country wanted to be the first to explore the unknown. Winning the Space Race would show the world who was the most powerful.

The First Satellites

Both the United States and the Soviet Union were working on satellites. In 1957, the Soviets were the first to launch a satellite into space. The satellite was named Sputnik. It was shaped like a globe. It had antennae sticking out. It orbited around the Earth for three weeks. It sent radio signals back to Earth. Then, the batteries ran down. Sputnik fell back to Earth after a couple of months.

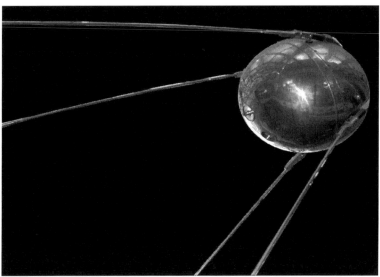

The first U.S. satellite was Explorer 1. It was launched into space in 1958. It was shaped like a missile. Explorer 1 carried science instruments. Its job was to measure the radiation in Earth's orbit. It sent information back to Earth. Explorer 1 stayed in orbit until 1970.

1. Underline the sentence that tells what winning the Space Race would show the world.
2. Underline the sentence that tells who was first to launch a satellite into space.
3. Underline the sentence that tells when Explorer 1 was launched.

Name_____ Date_____

Answer the questions with complete sentences.

1. What was the new conflict after World War II called?

   _____

   _____

2. What did each country in the Space Race want?

   _____

   _____

3. Who was the first to launch a satellite into space?

   _____

   _____

4. When was the U.S. satellite Explorer 1 launched into space?

   _____

   _____

5. What did Explorer 1 do while it was in orbit?

   _____

   _____

Story 11

NASA

The U.S. government was upset about Sputnik. The Soviets were ahead in the Space Race. It made the United States look bad. American scientists were working hard on the space program. But they didn't have enough support from the government.

In 1958, President Eisenhower created the National Aeronautics and Space Administration (NASA). NASA's purpose was space exploration. Congress gave NASA money to build a spacecraft. The U.S. wanted to win the Space Race!

The First Man in Space

The next part of the race was to get a man into space. On April 12, 1961, Yuri Gagarin became the first man to orbit the Earth. He was a Soviet cosmonaut. His flight lasted 108 minutes. He made a little over one orbit around the Earth. Then, he landed safely. Gagarin became a hero in the Soviet Union.

The U.S. was close behind. On May 5, 1961, Alan Shepard became the first American in space. He was on the spacecraft Freedom 7. Shepard's flight was only 15 minutes. He did not get into orbit around the Earth. In February 1962, John Glenn was the first American to orbit the Earth. He was on the spacecraft Friendship 7.

1. Underline the sentence that tells what President Eisenhower created.
2. Underline the sentence that tells who was the first man to orbit the Earth.
3. Underline the sentence that tells who was the first American in space.

Name_____ Date_____

Answer the questions with complete sentences.

1. What did President Eisenhower create in 1958?

   _____

   _____

2. What was NASA's purpose?

   _____

   _____

3. Who was the first man to orbit the Earth?

   _____

   _____

4. Who was the first American in space?

   _____

   _____

5. Who was the first American to orbit the Earth?

   _____

   _____

The Race to the Moon!

In 1961, John F. Kennedy was president of the United States. He was very unhappy the U.S. was behind in the space race. President Kennedy made a speech to Congress. He said before the end of the decade, the U.S. should land a man on the moon! He got money from Congress to help make this happen. It was the beginning of the Apollo Moon program.

Gemini was a two-man spacecraft. It was created by NASA to help astronauts get ready to land on the moon. There were 10 crews that flew missions on Gemini. The astronauts got to practice being in space. They did tests and solved problems. On Gemini 4, astronaut Ed White did the first space walk. On Gemini 7, astronauts were in space for two weeks. On some missions, the astronauts practiced connecting two spacecraft. The Gemini missions were flown in 1965 and 1966.

Scientists used information from the Gemini program to build the Apollo spacecraft. Apollo 11 was the mission to go to the moon. Astronauts Neil Armstrong, Buzz Aldrin, and Michael Collins were on this mission. On July 20, 1969, Neil Armstrong and Buzz Aldrin became the first humans to land on the moon! They were in a lunar module called the Eagle. Then, Neil Armstrong became the first person to walk on the moon! He said, "That's one small step for a man, one giant leap for mankind."

The End of the Space Race

After landing on the moon, America jumped ahead in the space race. By 1975, the space race was over. The U.S. and the Soviet Union started working together on the space program.

1. Underline the sentence that tells what President Kennedy said in his speech to Congress.

2. Underline the sentence that tells why the Gemini spacecraft was created.

3. Underline the sentence that tells what happened on July 20, 1969.

Name_____ Date_____

Answer the questions with complete sentences.

1. What did President Kennedy say in his speech to Congress?

   _____

   _____

2. Why was the Gemini spacecraft created?

   _____

   _____

3. Who were the Apollo 11 astronauts?

   _____

   _____

4. What happened on July 20, 1969?

   _____

   _____

5. Who was the first person to walk on the moon?

   _____

   _____

Name_____ Date_____

Complete each sentence with a word from the box.

launched	orbit	spacecraft
exploration	conflict	walk
cosmonaut	satellites	module

1. After World War II, there was a new _____ called the Cold War.

2. Both the U.S. and the Soviet Union were working on _____.

3. Sputnik was the first satellite _____ into space.

4. NASA's purpose was space _____.

5. Yuri Gagarin was a Soviet _____.

6. John Glenn was the first American to _____ the Earth.

7. Gemini was a two-man _____.

8. The lunar _____ was called the Eagle.

9. Neil Armstrong was the first person to _____ on the moon.

Read each completed sentence to make sure it makes sense.

Name_____ Date_____

Write two or more sentences about each topic.

Sputnik

NASA

Apollo 11

The Civil Rights Movement: Part 1

Story 12

Civil rights are the basic rights of all citizens. They should be guaranteed by the government. Civil rights should protect all citizens from being treated unfairly. It means all people should have equality in education, employment, housing, transportation, and more. It means all people should be free to go to any public places. African Americans did not have these civil rights.

Jim Crow Laws

After the Civil War, it was the end of slavery. But the South still did not treat African Americans fairly. Southern states passed laws that separated black people from white people. These laws were known as "Jim Crow Laws." African Americans had to go to separate schools, churches, restaurants, stores, and other public places. They had to use separate restrooms. There were signs everywhere that said, "Whites Only" or "Colored." These signs told African Americans where they could and could not go.

It was against the law for black people to marry white people. Laws were also passed that made it hard for African Americans to vote.

Northern states did not have Jim Crow Laws. It was easier for African Americans to live in the North. But there was still discrimination based on race. Many African Americans were tired of being treated so badly. They formed groups to fight for racial equality. Protests started in the 1950s. It was the beginning of the modern-day Civil Rights Movement.

1. Underline the two sentences that tell what it means for all people to have civil rights.
2. Underline the sentence that tells what kind of laws southern states passed.
3. Underline the sentence that tells why African Americans formed groups to fight for racial equality.

Name_____ Date_____

Answer the questions with complete sentences.

1. What does it mean for all people to have civil rights?

   _____

   _____

2. What kind of laws did southern states pass?

   _____

   _____

3. What did African Americans have to do because of Jim Crow Laws?

   _____

   _____

4. Why was it easier for African Americans to live in the North?

   _____

   _____

5. Why did African Americans form groups to fight for racial equality?

   _____

   _____

Name_____   Date_____

Story 12

Rosa Parks

Rosa Parks lived in Montgomery, Alabama. In Alabama, African Americans had to sit in the back of the city bus. Sometimes the white section of the bus got full. Then, African Americans had to give their seats to white passengers. On December 1, 1955, Rosa got on the bus after work. She sat in the front row of the "colored section." The "white section" of the bus was full. A white man got on the bus. He needed a seat. The bus driver asked Rosa to give up her seat. She said no! It took a lot of courage for Rosa to stay in her seat. Rosa Parks was arrested and fined $10.

Rosa Parks' arrest led to the Montgomery Bus Boycott. African Americans in Montgomery refused to ride the public buses. They would not ride a bus until they had equal rights The boycott was the first huge civil rights protest. About 40,000 African Americans stopped riding the bus. On December 20, 1956, the Supreme Court passed a law. Montgomery had to integrate their buses. The boycott was over. It had lasted 381 days! Later, Rosa Parks became known as "the mother of the civil rights movement."

The white citizens of Montgomery were not happy. They did not want integrated buses. African Americans were attacked at bus stops. Members of the Ku Klux Klan bombed African American churches. They bombed the homes of African American leaders. It took awhile for the violence to end.

1. Underline the sentence that tells what happened to Rosa Parks after she stayed in her seat.
2. Underline the sentence that tells how many African Americans stopped riding the bus.
3. Underline the sentence that tells who bombed African American churches.

Name_____ Date_____

Answer the questions with complete sentences.

1. What did Rosa Parks say when the bus driver asked her to give up her seat?

   _____

   _____

2. What happened to Rosa after she stayed in her seat?

   _____

   _____

3. What did African Americans do during the Montgomery Bus Boycott?

   _____

   _____

4. How many African Americans stopped riding the bus?

   _____

   _____

5. Who bombed African American churches?

   _____

   _____

Name _____ Date _____

Story 12

Dr. Martin Luther King, Jr.

In 1955, Dr. Martin Luther King, Jr. was living in Montgomery, Alabama. King was a popular African American minister. He was upset by Rosa Parks' arrest. He started the Montgomery Bus Boycott. During the boycott, King was arrested. His house was bombed. But he did not give up.

After that, he became the leader of the Civil Rights Movement. King did not believe in violence. He led non-violent marches and protests. He fought for the rights of all people. King believed the world should be colorblind. He thought a person's civil rights should not depend on skin color.

Dr. King was famous for his powerful speeches. King's speeches inspired many people. With King as its leader, the civil rights movement grew. He encouraged people to stand up for their rights.

The First Sit-In

In the South, most restaurants and lunch counters would not serve black people. Four African American college students decided to change that.

On February 1, 1960, the students sat down at a "white-only" lunch counter. They were at the Woolworth store in Greensboro, North Carolina. The young men ordered lunch. They were asked to leave. The students stayed in their seats. They sat there quietly and peacefully. They were waiting to be served. They came back every day. Other students joined them over the next few months. This protest was called a "sit-in." Soon, other peaceful sit-ins were happening across the South. In July of 1960, Woolworth served African American customers for the first time.

1. Underline the two sentences that tell what happened to King during the Montgomery Bus Boycott.
2. Underline the sentence that tells what happened on February 1, 1960.
3. Underline the sentence that tells what the protest at the Woolworth lunch counter was called.

Name_____ Date_____

Answer the questions with complete sentences.

1. What happened to Dr. Martin Luther King, Jr. during the Montgomery Bus Boycott?

   _____

   _____

2. What did Dr. King encourage people to do?

   _____

   _____

3. Where were the college students when they sat down at a "white-only" lunch counter?

   _____

   _____

4. What did the students do after they were asked to leave?

   _____

   _____

5. What was the protest at Woolworth's lunch counter called?

   _____

   _____

Name_____ Date_____

Complete each sentence with a word from the box.

courage	bombed	separated
riding	non-violent	white-only
citizens	racial	sit-in

1. Civil rights are the basic rights of all _____.

2. Jim Crow Laws _____ black people from white people.

3. African Americans formed groups to fight for _____ equality.

4. It took a lot of _____ for Rosa Parks to stay in her seat.

5. About 40,000 African Americans stopped _____ the bus.

6. Members of the Ku Klux Klan _____ African American churches.

7. Dr. Martin Luther King, Jr. led _____ marches and protests.

8. Four African America students sat down at a _____ lunch counter.

9. The protest at the Woolworth lunch counter was called a _____.

Read each completed sentence to make sure it makes sense.

Name_____ Date_____

Write two or more sentences about each topic.

Jim Crow Laws

_____
_____
_____

Rosa Parks

_____
_____
_____

Dr. Martin Luther King, Jr.

_____
_____
_____

Name_____ Date_____

The Civil Rights Movement: Part 2

Story 13

Throughout the 1960s, many brave people fought for civil rights. There were hundreds of protests, marches, sit-ins, and demonstrations. Some were peaceful. Some turned violent. The civil rights movement grew to include thousands of people across the country.

Freedom Riders

Freedom Riders were protesting segregation in southern bus stations. They were groups of black and white civil rights activists. On May 14, 1961, the first group of Freedom Riders were on a Greyhound bus. They were in rural Alabama. An angry mob of about 200 white people surrounded the bus. The mob threw rocks and bricks at the bus. They slashed the tires. Someone threw a bomb through a broken window. The bus burst into flames. The passengers hurried off the burning bus. They were beaten by the mob.

That same day, a group of Freedom Riders were in Birmingham, Alabama. They went into a whites-only waiting room at a bus station. They were badly beaten by another angry mob. There was more violence at other bus stations.

There were photos and news reports about the attacks. The news reports told how bad things were for African Americans in the South. After this, more people were willing to risk their lives. They wanted to fight for racial equality. More than 400 Freedom Riders continued to ride buses. This went on for seven months. In the fall of 1961, a law was passed. Southern bus stations could no longer be segregated.

1. Underline the sentence that tells what Freedom Riders were protesting.
2. Underline the sentence that tells what happened after the passengers hurried off the burning bus.
3. Underline the sentence that tells what the news report told about the attacks.

Name_____ Date_____

Answer the questions with complete sentences.

1. What were the Freedom Riders protesting?

   _____
   _____

2. Describe what happened after an angry mob surrounded the Freedom Riders' bus.

   _____
   _____

3. Why did another group of Freedom Riders get badly beaten by an angry mob in Birmingham, Alabama?

   _____
   _____

4. What did news reports tell about the attacks on the bus?

   _____
   _____

5. What changed after a law was passed in the fall of 1961?

   _____
   _____

Story 13

March on Washington

On August 28, 1963, the famous March on Washington took place. Dr. Martin Luther King, Jr. helped plan the march. Over 250,000 protesters met in Washington, D.C. They marched peacefully for jobs and freedom. The protesters wanted job equality for African Americans. They wanted freedom for all people.

The marchers gathered at the Lincoln Memorial. There were more than 3,000 members of the press at the event. Well-known civil rights leaders gave speeches throughout the day. The last to speak was Dr. King. He gave his famous "I Have a Dream" speech. Many people were deeply moved by his speech. This peaceful protest changed how America felt about civil rights. Many white people across the country now gave their support.

The Civil Rights Act of 1964

President Johnson signed the Civil Rights Act into law on July 2, 1964. This ended the Jim Crow Laws in the South. Segregation was no longer allowed in public places. This included restaurants, parks, theaters, sporting events, hotels, and other places of business. People could not be refused service based on their skin color. It was illegal to not hire someone because of their race, gender, or religion.

This was a very important law for the civil rights movement. But it did not end the racial problems in the South.

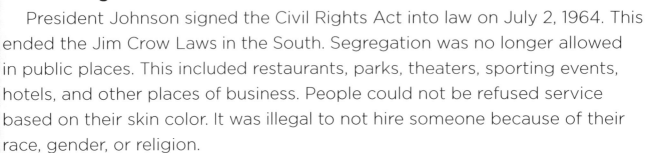

1. Underline the sentence that tells when the March on Washington took place.
2. Underline the sentence that tells what speech Dr. King gave.
3. Underline the two sentences that tell what changed after the Civil Rights Act was signed into law.

Name_____ Date_____

Answer the questions with complete sentences.

1. When did the March on Washington take place?

   _____

   _____

2. How many protesters met in Washington, D.C.?

   _____

   _____

3. Why were the protesters marching?

   _____

   _____

4. What speech did Dr. King give at the march?

   _____

   _____

5. What changed after the Civil Rights Act was signed into law?

   _____

   _____

Story 13

Bloody Sunday

On Sunday March 7, 1965, 600 civil rights activists gathered in Selma, Alabama. They planned to march 54 miles from Selma to Montgomery. The march was to protest the killing of an African American protester. The march was also about voting rights. The state of Alabama made it hard for African Americans to vote.

The marchers began to cross the Edmund Pettus bridge in Selma. A row of state troopers was there to stop them. The troopers knocked the marchers to the ground. They beat them with clubs. They shot tear gas into the crowd. Men on horses chased the marchers back across the bridge. They hit people with whips. The protesters screamed and cried in pain. But they did not fight back. The marchers remained non-violent.

The attack on the protesters was shown on television. Many Americans were shocked and upset. The attack became known as Bloody Sunday. President Johnson took action after the march. He asked Congress to pass the Voting Rights Act of 1965. It was signed into law in August of 1965.

Assassination of Dr. Martin Luther King, Jr.

April 4, 1968 was a sad day for America and the world. Dr. Martin Luther King, Jr. was shot and killed in Memphis, Tennessee. He was only 39 years old. His death caused riots and protests across the country. The civil rights movement had lost its leader. But the movement went on without him. The fight for equal rights continues today.

1. Underline the two sentences that tell why the protesters were marching from Selma to Montgomery.
2. Underline the sentence that tells what action President Johnson took after the march.
3. Underline the sentence that tells why April 4, 1968 was a sad day for America and the world.

Name_____ Date_____

Answer the questions with complete sentences.

1. Why were the protesters marching from Selma to Montgomery?

   _____

   _____

2. Name three things that the state troopers did to the marchers.

   _____

   _____

3. What did the attack in Selma become known as?

   _____

   _____

4. What action did President Johnson take after the march?

   _____

   _____

5. Why was April 4, 1968 a sad day for America and the world?

   _____

   _____

Name_____ Date_____

Complete each sentence with a word from the box.

peacefully	continued	allowed
press	segregation	shocked
troopers	across	mob

1. Freedom Riders were protesting _____ in southern bus stations.

2. An angry _____ threw rocks and bricks at the bus.

3. More than 400 Freedom Riders _____ to ride buses.

4. Protesters marched _____ for jobs and freedom.

5. More than 3,000 members of the _____ were at the March on Washington.

6. Segregation was no longer _____ in public places.

7. State _____ beat the marchers with clubs.

8. Many Americans were _____ and upset by the attack on the protesters.

9. Dr. King's death caused riots and protests _____ the country.

Read each completed sentence to make sure it makes sense.

Name_____ Date_____

Write two or more sentences about each topic.

Freedom Riders

_____
_____
_____

March on Washington

_____
_____
_____

Bloody Sunday

_____
_____
_____

The Sixties

Story 14

The 1960s was a decade of revolution and great change in America. It was a time of hippies, peace, love, and rock and roll. It was also a time of marches, protests, violence, and war. There were new kinds of music and new ways of dressing. Young people had a new sense of freedom. At the same time, women and African-Americans were fighting for equal rights. Famous leaders were assassinated. And a war was going on in Vietnam.

Hippies

Hippies were young men and women who "dropped out" of society. They did not want to live like their parents' generation. They did not want to work at "regular" jobs. The women wore their hair long. The

men also had long hair and many grew beards. Both men and women wore loose, flowing clothes in bright colors. Some of their clothes were tie-dyed and had crazy patterns. Some people called hippies "flower children." Many of these young people lived together in large houses or communes. Hippies just wanted a relaxed life of freedom, peace, and love.

Sixties Music

Music in the sixties was revolutionary. New types of blues, folk, and rock music were created. The music was often loud and joyful. But it could also be sad and angry. American teenagers were crazy for the Beatles. The Beatles were British. They brought modern pop music to America. Protest singers like Bob Dylan and Joan Baez sang about changing the world. Sixties music told the story of how young people felt.

1. Underline the sentence that tells what women and African-Americans were doing in the 1960s.
2. Underline the sentence that tells what kind of life hippies wanted.
3. Underline the sentence that tells what the Beatles brought to America.

Name_____ Date_____

Answer the questions with complete sentences.

1. What were women and African-Americans doing during the 1960s?

   _____

   _____

2. Name two things that hippies did not want to do.

   _____

   _____

3. What kind of life did hippies want?

   _____

   _____

4. What did the Beatles bring to America?

   _____

   _____

5. Who sang about changing the world?

   _____

   _____

Assassinations

There was a darker part to the sixties. Three important American leaders were assassinated. On November 22, 1963, President John F. Kennedy was shot and killed in Dallas, Texas. He was riding through downtown Dallas. He was in an open car. He was smiling and waving to the crowds. Suddenly, the President was hit by two bullets. He died on the way to the hospital. The country was shocked and heartbroken! President Kennedy's death was just the beginning of much more violence to come.

On April 4, 1968, Martin Luther King, Jr. was assassinated. He had been the leader of the Civil Rights Movement since the 1950s. His death caused riots across the country. Shortly after that, on June 5, 1968, Robert Kennedy was shot. He died the next day. Robert Kennedy was President Kennedy's brother. He was running for president.

Vietnam and the Anti-War Movement

The Vietnam War was the most unpopular war in American history. It tore the country apart. By 1967, there were over 500,000 American troops in Vietnam. There were marches and protests against the war. In 1969, 250,000 people gathered peacefully in Washington, D.C. It was the largest anti-war demonstration in American history. The protesters were asking for America to get out of Vietnam.

1. Underline the sentence that tells what happened on November 22, 1963.
2. Underline the sentence that tells who Martin Luther King, Jr. was.
3. Underline the sentence that tells what the protesters were asking for.

Name_____ Date_____

Answer the questions with complete sentences.

1. Where and when was President John F. Kennedy shot and killed?

   _____
   _____

2. Who was Martin Luther King, Jr. and when was he assassinated?

   _____
   _____

3. Who was Robert Kennedy and when was he shot?

   _____
   _____

4. How many people were gathered in Washington, D.C. in 1969?

   _____
   _____

5. What were the protesters in Washington, D.C. asking for?

   _____
   _____

Story 14

Many college students were against the war. On May 4, 1970, there was an anti-war protest at Kent State University in Ohio. The National Guard opened fire on the unarmed students. Four students were killed. Nine more were wounded. This caused more protests at colleges. It also caused more violence and death.

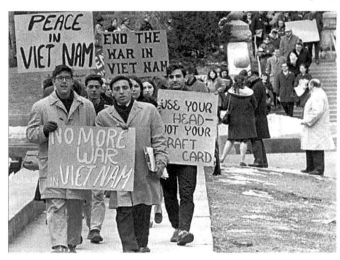

The Women's Movement

In the 1960s, women still did not have some of the same rights as men. Women could not work at certain jobs. Women did not have equal pay. Men made more money doing the same job. Many women wanted to be more than a housewife and mother. They wanted interesting careers. Women of all ages marched and protested. They wanted a change. In 1966, the National Organization for Women (NOW) was formed. NOWs main goal was to get the Equal Rights Amendment (ERA) passed. The ERA guarantees equal legal rights for all women and men. Congress passed the amendment in 1972. But some states have still not agreed to it.

The War on Poverty

After President Kennedy was killed, Lyndon Johnson became president. Johnson declared a War on Poverty. He wanted to help end poverty in America. He created programs to "give poor people a hand up, not a handout." Two important programs were Medicare and Medicaid. These programs help seniors and low-income people pay for health care. Another program, Head Start, helps preschoolers prepare for school. The Job Corps trains people for over 100 different kinds of jobs. All of these programs are still helping people today.

1. Underline the the sentence that tells who opened fire on unarmed students.
2. Underline the sentence that tells what the ERA guarantees.
3. Underline the sentence that tells why President Johnson declared a War on Poverty.

Name_____ Date_____

Answer the questions with complete sentences.

1. What happened at Kent State University in Ohio?

   _____

   _____

2. What organization was formed in 1966?

   _____

   _____

3. What does the ERA guarantee?

   _____

   _____

4. Why did President Johnson declare a War on Poverty?

   _____

   _____

5. How do the Medicare and Medicaid programs help people?

   _____

   _____

Name_____ Date_____

Complete each sentence with a word from the box.

assassinated	revolutionary	against
heartbroken	hippies	trains
preschoolers	women	communes

1. The 1960s was a time of _____ , peace, love, and rock and roll.

2. Many hippies lived together in large houses or _____ .

3. Music in the sixties was _____ .

4. Three important American leaders were _____ .

5. After President Kennedy was killed, the country was shocked and _____ .

6. There were marches and protests _____ the war.

7. Men made more money than _____ doing the same job.

8. Head Start helps _____ prepare for school.

9. Job Corps _____ people for over 100 different jobs.

Read each completed sentence to make sure it makes sense.

Name_____ Date_____

Write two or more sentences about each topic.

Hippies

_____
_____
_____
_____

Sixties Music

_____
_____
_____
_____

The War on Poverty

_____
_____
_____
_____

WORDS TO KNOW

Story 1   The Industrial Revolution

assembly line	manufactured	wages
factories	mass-produce	weave
improve	survive	working conditions
Industrial Revolution	system	worthwhile
independence	textile	

Story 2   Immigration

ancestors	dingy	permission	survival
decision	immigrants	poverty	sweatshops
desperate	immigration	religion	tenements
destroyed	medical exam	religious	widespread
determination	passage		

Story 3   World War I (1914-1918)

advantage	declared	official	telegram
allies	empire	passenger	tension
chain of events	enemy	repair	torpedoes
competed	furious	submarines	warned
damages			

Story 4   Women's Right to Vote

Amendment to the Constitution	picketed
antislavery movement	protest
demanded	Quaker
dependent	suffrage
document	suffragettes
obey	

WORDS TO KNOW

Story 5   The Roaring Twenties

afford	fancy	nickname
broadcast	fashion	renaissance
corsets	flappers	segregation
credit	hardships	successful industries
economy	hemlines	suspenders
entertainment	inventions	

Story 6   Hollywood and the Movies!

American culture	dramatic facial expressions	escape
average	filmmakers	mustache
body language	glamour	talented
bowler hat	glamorous	Technicolor
character	Great Depression	plot

Story 7   The Great Depression

desperate	protected	shares of stock
drought	restore	solve
economic depression	riots	stock market
invested		

Story 8   World War II in Europe

concentration camps	dictators	invaded
deadliest	Holocaust	

Story 9   World War II in the Pacific

aircraft carriers	atomic bomb	battleships	resources

WORDS TO KNOW

Story 10 — America Loves Television

advertise	commercials	fascinated	networks
candidate			

Story 11 — The Space Race

actual	conflict	launch	satellites
aeronautics	cosmonaut	orbit	spacecraft
antennae	explore	radiation	spied
competition			

Story 12 — The Civil Rights Movement: Part 1

arrest	encouraged	inspired	sit-in
boycott	guaranteed	integrate	racial equality
discrimination			

Story 13 — The Civil Rights Movement: Part 2

activists	protesters	risk	segregation
gender			

Story 14 — The Sixties

anti-war	communes	revolution	revolutionary
assassination	demonstration		

WORDS TO KNOW: PEOPLE & PLACES

Story 1 — The Industrial Revolution

PEOPLE
Henry Ford

Story 2 — Immigration

PEOPLE
European Immigrants
Chinese Immigrants

PLACES
Ellis Island
New York City
Hudson River
New Jersey
Great Britain
Ireland
Germany
Italy
Russia
Poland

Story 3 — World War i (1914-1918)

PEOPLE
Archduke Franz Ferdinand
President Woodrow Wilson

PLACES
France
Bosnia
Serbia
Mexico

Story 4 — Women's Right to Vote

PEOPLE
Elizabeth Cady Stanton
Susan B. Anthony
Lucretia Mott

PLACES
Seneca Falls, New York

Story 5 — The Roaring Twenties

PEOPLE
Louis Armstrong
Duke Ellington
Bessie Smith
Langston Hughes
Zora Neale Hurston
James Baldwin

PLACES
Harlem

WORDS TO KNOW: PEOPLE & PLACES

Story 6   Hollywood and the Movies!

PEOPLE
D.W. Griffith
Charlie Chaplin
Mary Pickford
Clark Gable
Katherine Hepburn
Cary Grant
Fred Astaire
Ginger Rogers
James Cagney
Humphrey Bogart
Shirley Temple

PLACES
Hollywood
Los Angeles

Story 7   The Great Depression

PEOPLE
Franklin Delano Roosevelt

PLACES
Southern Great Plains
Kansas
Oklahoma
Texas
New Mexico
Colorado

Story 8   World War II in Europe

PEOPLE
Nazis
Benito Mussolini
Adolf Hitler

PLACES
Poland
Norway
Denmark

Story 9   World War II in the Pacific

PEOPLE
Emperor Hirohito (hear-oh-HEE-tow)
President Harry Truman

PLACES
Pearl Harbor, Hawaii
Japan
China
Southeast Asia
Midway Island
Iwo Jima (ee-WHO JEE-muh)
Hiroshima (huh-ROH-shuh-muh)
Nagasaki (nah-gah-SAH-kee)

WORDS TO KNOW: PEOPLE & PLACES

Story 10   America Loves Television

PEOPLE
Dwight Eisenhower

Story 11   The Space Race

PEOPLE
Yuri Gagarin
Alan Shepard
John Glenn
John F. Kennedy
Ed White
Neil Armstrong
Buzz Aldrin
Michael Collins

Story 12   The Civil Rights Movement: Part 1

PEOPLE
Rosa Parks
Dr. Martin Luther King, Jr.

PLACES
Montgomery, Alabama
Greensboro, North Carolina

Story 13   The Civil Rights Movement: Part 2

PEOPLE
President Lyndon Johnson

PLACES
Selma, Alabama
Edmund Pettus Bridge
Birmingham, Alabama
Washington, D.C.

Story 14   The Sixties

PEOPLE
The Beatles
Bob Dylan
Joan Baez
Robert Kennedy

PLACES
Dallas, Texas
Vietnam
Kent State University

ENRICHMENT IDEAS

The following higher-level thinking skills questions can be used as discussion starters or as extended learning writing assignments.

1. What do you think it would be like to work in an unsafe factory that was hot, dirty, and crowded?

2. How do you think immigrants should be treated when they first come to America?

3. Do you think America should have fought in World War I? Explain your answer.

4. Why do you think it took so long for women to get the right to vote?

5. What do you think is the most important thing that happened during the Roaring Twenties?

6. What is your favorite kind of movie and why?

7. If you were president during the Great Depression, what would you have done to help the country?

8. Do you think there is ever a good reason to drop an atomic bomb on an enemy? Explain your answer.

9. How would your life be affected if television had never been invented?

10. What do you think is the best thing about being an astronaut?

11. Do you think all people in America have equal rights today? Explain your answer.

12. Do you think sit-ins were a good way to protest? Explain your answer.

13. If you were alive during the 1960s, would you have protested against the Vietnam War? Explain your answer.

14. Do you think there should still be a War on Poverty? Why or why not?

ENRICHMENT IDEAS

Find out more...

- Find out more about how the Industrial Revolution changed America.

- Find out what country or countries your ancestors came from.

- Find out more about World War I submarines.

- Find out more about women's suffrage in the early 1900s.

- Find out more about popular radio programs during the 1920s.

- Find out more about the artists, writers, and musicians that were part of the Harlem Renaissance.

- Find out more about 1930s child star Shirley Temple.

- Find out more about what happened during the drought that caused the Dust Bowl.

- Find out more about Pearl Harbor, Hawaii.

- Find out more about what happened to Hiroshima and Nagasaki after the atomic bomb was dropped.

- Find out more about the shows that kids watched on TV during the 1950s.

- Find out more about the Apollo Moon program.

- Find out more about Freedom Riders.

- Find out more about the Vietnam War.

- Find out more about the music of the 1960s.

ANSWER KEY

Story 1
Page 5
1. Using textile mills to make cloth started the Industrial Revolution.
2. Soap, towels, dishes, glassware, hats, shoes, clothing, perfume and candy were all made in factories.
3. They wanted to work in factories.
4. Factory cities grew quickly and some became overcrowded.
5. The automobile and airplane opened up a whole new world of transportation.

Page 7
1. Products were made one at a time at home or in small workshops.
2. Products were made by machines. Workers came together in large buildings and ran the machines.
3. Henry Ford was the first to use a moving assembly line.
4. A different part of the car was added at each station.
5. It took 12 hours before and under two hours after.

Page 9
1. They could pay women less money.
2. The families needed the children's wages to survive.
3. The factory rooms were hot, dirty, crowded, and noisy, and the machines were unsafe.
4. Many workers got sick and some got injured or killed in accidents.
5. Labor unions gave workers a voice. They demanded better pay and safer working conditions.

Page 10
1. Revolution 2. factories 3. population 4. mass-produce
5. assembly 6. under 7. twice 8. safe 9. Labor

Story 2
Page 13
1. An immigrant is a person who leaves the country where they were born and comes to live in a new country.
2. They came from Great Britain, Ireland, Germany.
3. They leave because of war, poverty, and not being able to practice their religion.
4. They came for jobs and for religious freedom.
5. About 15 million immigrants came to America.

Page 15
1. It was on the Hudson River between New York and New Jersey.
2. They didn't know if they would be allowed to stay.
3. They had to get permission. They had to answer questions and get a medical exam.
4. Between 5,000 and 10,000 people came every day.
5. There was a limit on how many people could come to America from each country.

Page 17
1. There could be as many as 4,000 immigrants per block.
2. It had a small living room, a kitchen, and a tiny bedroom.
3. They had no skills and could not speak English.
4. They were dirty, dingy places with no windows.
5. They didn't like how they looked or talked.

Page 18
1. immigrants 2. poverty 3. spread 4. station 5. afraid 6. into
7. crowded 8. dingy 9. treated

Story 3
Page 21
1. Germany and Austria-Hungary were the main Central Powers. Great Britain, France, and Russia were the main Allied Powers.
2. Each country wanted to be the most powerful.
3. Allies are countries who are friends that help each other and fight together.
4. The Archduke and his wife were killed.
5. Germany took Austria-Hungary's side. Russia took Serbia's side.

Page 23
1. They declared war on July 28, 1914.
2. Germany declared war on Russia and France.
3. He did not want the U.S. to take sides in the war.
4. They loaned large sums of money to the Allied countries.
5. Machine guns, tanks, flamethrowers, and poison gas were new weapons.

Page 25
1. He warned them to stop sinking passenger ships and killing Americans.
2. It asked Mexico to join the Central Powers and fight against America.
3. America declared war in April of 1917.
4. America sent almost 2 million soldiers, food, supplies, and weapons.
5. The Allied Powers won the war.

Page 26
1. allies 2. tension 3. wife 4. declared 5. pilots 6. torpedoes
7. warned 8. telegram 9. advantage

Story 4
Page 29
1. Women have had the right to vote for about 100 years.
2. It gave all men, even African-Americans, the right to vote.
3. Men believed that women were not their equals.
4. Wives were often treated like property.
5. Women could not vote.

Page 31
1. Women's suffrage is the right of women to vote in an election.
2. Suffragettes were women who fought for the right to vote.
3. Their main goal was to get a law passed that allowed women to vote.
4. Men did not want women to vote.
5. They were treated badly. They were yelled at, got injured, and were sometimes sent to jail.

Page 33
1. Her husband supported her work to help women.
2. She was famous for giving speeches on women's rights.
3. They worked together for over 50 years.
4. It gives all women over the age of 21 the right to vote.
5. Women first voted in November of 1920.

ANSWER KEY

Page 34
1. vote 2. earn 3. brave 4. convention 5. protest 6. suffragettes
7. rights 8. working 9. first

Story 5
Page 37
1. They listened to new music, tried new dances, bought new clothes, and tried new entertainment.
2. There were lots of new jobs and both men and women were working.
3. Electric vacuum cleaners, refrigerators, and washing machines made life easier.
4. Men wore pinstriped suits, silk shirts, suspenders, bow ties, and black patent leather shoes.
5. The new dress styles were loose and comfortable, hemlines were above the knee, no more need for corsets.

Page 39
1. It cost $260.
2. Movies became popular.
3. It cost between 10 and 25 cents.
4. They broadcast music, the latest news, comedy shows, and dramas.
5. Baseball became popular.

Page 41
1. Women could vote. They could go to college, work, and learn to drive.
2. They were called flappers.
3. The Shimmy, The Turkey Trot, The Cake Walk, and The Bunny Hop were the crazy new dances.
4. African-Americans were treated very badly and segregation made life very difficult.
5. Louis Armstrong, Duke Ellington, Bessie Smith, Langston Hughes, Zora Neale Hurston, and James Baldwin became famous.

Page 42
1. afford 2. credit 3. Hemlines 4. average 5. movies 6. fancy
7. Jazz 8. wore 9. Renaissance

Story 6
Page 45
1. The weather was warm and sunny and there were plenty of wide open spaces.
2. The first motion picture cameras did not include sound.
3. The actors told the story with body language and dramatic facial expressions.
4. The plot of the story and what the actors said was written on the title cards.
5. It made them feel happy, sad, excited, or afraid.

Page 47
1. Charlie Chaplin and Mary Pickford were two of the most famous silent movie stars.
2. He had sad eyes and a small mustache. He wore a bowler hat, baggy pants, big shoes and carried a cane.
3. She was called "America's Sweetheart." She was known for her long, golden curls.
4. They were called "talkies."
5. It was a different kind of acting.

Page 49
1. It started in the 1920s and went through the 1950s.
2. An average of 700 movies were made each year.
3. About 100 million people went to the movies each week.
4. Clark Gable, Katherine Hepburn, Cary Grant, Fred Astaire, Ginger Rogers, James Cagney, Humphrey Bogart, and Shirley Temple were all famous movie stars.
5. *The Wizard of Oz* and *Gone with the Wind* are still famous today.

Page 50
1. perfect 2. silent 3. expressions 4. character 5. movies 6. sang
7. average 8. glamorous 9. escape

Story 7
Page 53
1. It started in 1929 and lasted through the end of the 1930s.
2. The stock market is a place where people can buy and sell shares of stock in a company.
3. When stock prices go up people make money. When they go down people lose money.
4. The stock market crashed.
5. They lost all their money.

Page 55
1. The customers lost all their money.
2. Over 9,000 banks closed.
3. They lost their jobs.
4. They had to walk from city to city. They had to sleep in tents or cardboard boxes or under bridges.
5. They waited in line to get a little bit to eat.

Page 57
1. Kansas, Oklahoma, Texas, New Mexico, and Colorado became known as the Dust Bowl.
2. The soil dried up and turned to dust and the crops died.
3. Over 2 million people left.
4. He wanted the government to help people who had lost their jobs and farms.
5. Millions of jobs were created building roads and bridges. Farmers were put to work planting trees.

Page 58
1. economic 2. crashed 3. money 4. riots 5. companies
6. hungry 7. drought 8. dried 9. winds

Story 8
Page 61
1. Germany, Italy, and Japan were Axis Powers. Great Britain, France, and the Soviet Union were Allied Powers.
2. It lasted six years.
3. They promised jobs and a better life.
4. Benito Mussolini was the dictator of Italy. Adolf Hitler became the dictator of Germany.
5. They made a deal to fight together if there was a war.

Page 63
1. He thought they couldn't be trusted. He thought they caused Germany to lose the war and that they were the cause of Germany's problems.
2. Hitler's goal was to control all of Europe.

ANSWER KEY

3. Hitler invaded Poland.
4. They promised to help if Poland was attacked by Germany.
5. They had an excellent Army and Air Force. They had the best military planes and tanks.

Page 65
1. Italy joined with Germany on June 10, 1940.
2. They were sent to concentration camps.
3. Everyone was killed right away.
4. Over 6 million Jewish people died in the camps.
5. The Allied forces won the war.

Page 66
1. deadliest 2. Dictators 3. Germany 4. Jewish 5. control
6. declared 7. concentration 8. sick 9. Allied

Story 9
Page 69
1. It started at the end of 1941.
2. Emperor Hirohito was the ruler of Japan.
3. Japan invaded China.
4. They destroyed cities and farms and killed thousands of Chinese people.
5. They wanted to rule the world.

Page 71
1. An important U.S. Naval base was at Pearl Harbor.
2. It took place on December 7, 1941.
3. They dropped their bombs on the harbor and the airfield at the same time.
4. Twenty-one ships were sunk or damaged. Over 180 fighter planes were destroyed.
5. America declared war on Japan.

Page 73
1. They were sent to fight the Japanese.
2. They were afraid too many American soldiers would be killed.
3. It was the atomic bomb.
4. It was dropped on August 6, 1945.
5. Another atomic bomb was dropped on Nagasaki.

Page 74
1. population 2. ruler 3. invaded 4. destroy 5. less 6. next
7. atomic 8. decided 9. surrendered

Story 10
Page 77
1. They cost about $500.
2. Half of all American homes had TV sets.
3. They were filmed in black and white.
4. Watching TV had a huge effect on the American way of life.
5. Millions of people were watching the same show as the same time.

Page 79
1. NBC, CBS, and ABC were the three major networks.
2. It started at about 10:00 each morning. The networks signed off at about 11:00 every night.
3. Kids shows, soap operas, game shows, and talk shows were on during the day.

4. The news, variety shows, westerns, comedies, and dramas were on in the evening.
5. They could reach millions of people at the same time.

Page 81
1. They were broadcast live.
2. Dwight Eisenhower was the first candidate.
3. I Love Lucy was the most popular comedy.
4. Over 30 Westerns were on each week.
5. By 1965, 94% had TV sets.

Page 83
1. cost 2. filmed 3. television 4. networks 5. Commercials
6. advertising 7. viewers 8. Westerns 9. daily

Story 11
Page 85
1. It was called the Cold War.
2. They wanted the best space technology. They wanted to be the first to explore the unknown.
3. The Soviets were the first to launch a satellite into space.
4. It was launched in 1958.
5. Explorer 1 measured the radiation in Earth's orbit and it sent the information back to Earth.

Page 87
1. He created the National Aeronautics and Space Administration (NASA).
2. Its purpose was space exploration.
3. Yuri Gagarin was the first man to orbit the Earth.
4. Alan Shepard was the first American in space.
5. John Glenn was the first American to orbit the Earth.

Page 89
1. Kennedy said before the end of the decade, the U.S. should land a man on the moon.
2. It was created by NASA to help astronauts get ready to land on the moon.
3. Neil Armstrong, Buzz Aldrin, and Michael Collins were the Apollo 11 astronauts.
4. Armstrong and Aldrin became the first humans to land on the moon.
5. Neil Armstrong was the first person to walk on the moon.

Page 90
1. conflict 2. satellites 3. launched 4. exploration 5. cosmonaut
6. orbit 7. spacecraft 8. module 9. walk

Story 12
Page 93
1. It means all people should have equality in education, employment, housing, and transportation. All people should be able to go to any public place.
2. They passed laws that separated black people from white people.
3. They had to go to separate schools, churches, restaurants, stores and other public places. They had to use separate restrooms.
4. The north did not have Jim Crow Laws.
5. They were tired of being treated so badly.

Daily Literacy Activities: 19th Century American History © Remedia Publications

ANSWER KEY

Page 95
1. She said no.
2. She got arrested and fined $10.
3. They refused to ride the city buses.
4. About 40,000 stopped riding the bus.
5. The Ku Klux Klan bombed the churches.

Page 97
1. He was arrested and his house was bombed.
2. He encouraged people to stand up for their rights.
3. They were at the Woolworth store in Greensboro, North Carolina.
4. They stayed in their seats. They sat quietly and peacefully.
5. It was called a "sit-in."

Page 98
1. citizens 2. separated 3. racial 4. courage 5. riding 6. bombed 7. non-violent 8. white-only 9. sit-in

Story 13
Page 101
1. They were protesting segregation in Southern bus stations.
2. The mob threw rock and bricks at the bus. They slashed the tires and someone threw a bomb through a broken window.
3. They went into a whites-only waiting room in a bus station.
4. They told how bad things were for the African Americans in the South.
5. Southern bus stations could no longer be segregated.

Page 103
1. The march took place on August 28,1963.
2. Over 250,000 protesters met in Washington, D.C.
3. They were marching for jobs and freedom
4. He gave his famous "I Have a Dream" speech.
5. The Jim Crow Laws were ended in the South. Segregation was no longer allowed in public places.

Page 105
1. They were protesting the killing of an African American protester and marching for voter rights.
2. The troopers beat them with clubs, shot tear gas into the crowd, chased them on horses and whipped them.
3. It became known as Bloody Sunday.
4. He asked Congress to pass the Voting Rights Act of 1965.
5. Dr. Martin Luther King, Jr. was shot and killed in Memphis, TN.

Page 106
1. segregation 2. mob 3. continued 4. peacefully 5. press 6. allowed 7. troopers 8. shocked 9. across

Story 14
Page 109
1. They were fighting for equal rights.
2. They did not want to live like their parents' generation. They did not want to work at regular jobs.
3. Hippies wanted a relaxed life of freedom, peace, and love.
4. The brought modern pop music.
5. Bob Dylan and Joan Baez sang about changing the world.

Page 111
1. President Kennedy was shot and killed on November 22, 1963 in Dallas, Texas.
2. Martin Luther King, Jr. was the leader of the Civil Rights movement. He was assassinated on April 4, 1968.
3. Robert Kennedy was President Kennedy's brother. He was shot on June 5, 1968.
4. There were 250,000 people gathered in Washington D.C.
5. They were asking for America to get out of Vietnam.

Page 113
1. Four students were killed and nine more were wounded.
2. The National Organization for Women was formed.
3. It guarantees equal legal rights for all women and men.
4. He wanted to help end poverty in America.
5. These programs help seniors and low-income people pay for health care.

Page 114
1. hippies 2. communes 3. revolutionary 4. assassinated 5. heartbroken 6. against 7. women 8. preschoolers 9. trains

NOTES

NOTES

A NEW ONE-OF-A-KIND SERIES!
Helping Struggling Readers Become Literate in American History

DAILY LITERACY ACTIVITIES
A Unique Concept Using Daily Reading Lessons to Teach American History

INTEREST LEVEL 4-12 **READING LEVEL 4-5**

Each Book Includes:
- 14 Literacy Study Units
- High-Interest, Easy-to-Read Stories
- Step-by-step, Customizable Daily Lessons
- Pre-Reading Strategies
- Enrichment Ideas

Grab your student's attention with exciting, easy-to-read stories written specifically for students performing below grade level. Daily lessons guide students to carefully read each story, answer questions that test comprehension, and then write about what they've learned.

Each book contains 14 important historical topics presented in eight-page study units. Each unit contains a three-page, fact-filled story complete with historical images on each page accompanied by five skill-based reading and writing activity pages. The format of the study units is flexible and user-friendly – perfect for differentiated instruction. Students can work at their own pace according to their ability level. Daily practice helps struggling readers become more literate in American history while improving essential reading and writing skills. 128+ pages per book.

Early American History
Learn about how the British colonies of America became the United States of America.

Topics include:
- The First Americans
- The 13 Colonies
- The Fight for Freedom
- Forming a New Government

19th Century American History
Learn about how westward expansion grew America but destroyed the Native American way of life.

Topics include:
- Settling the West
- Slavery in America
- The Civil War
- Reconstruction & Segregation

20th Century American History
Learn about how the industrial age first brought prosperity and then economic depression while many people struggled for personal liberties.

Topics include:
- World Wars I and II
- The Great Depression
- The Space Race
- The Civil Rights Movement

This series takes students on a compelling journey through American History!

8-Page Study Units on 14 Important Historical Topics per Book

PREVIEW SAMPLES & ORDER ONLINE AT **WWW.REMEDIA.COM** | FAX PURCHASE ORDERS TO **877-661-9901**